Rube Goldberg vs. The Machine Age

Rube Goldberg

Rube Goldberg, 1. having a fantastically complicated, improvised appearance: *a Rube Goldberg arrangement of flasks and test tubes.* 2. deviously complex and impractical: *a Rube Goldberg scheme for reducing taxes.* — THE RANDOM HOUSE DICTIONARY OF THE ENGLISH LANGUAGE.

vs. The Machine Age

A Retrospective Exhibition of His Work
With Memoirs and Annotations

EDITED BY CLARK KINNAIRD

Ralph Hollenbeck, Research Associate

HASTINGS HOUSE   *Publishers*   New York

Published simultaneously in Canada
by Saunders, of Toronto, Ltd., Don Mills, Ontario
SBN: 8038 — 6305-5
Library of Congress Catalogue Card Number: 68-31689

Printed in the United States of America

Drawing in half-title page, The Fountains of
Rome, from *Rube Goldberg's Guide to Europe,* with
text by Sam Boal (Vanguard Press, 1954).

Contents

Introduction

More than ten thousand introductions to the works of Reuben Lucius Goldberg have been published. At least 99 99/100 have been in the purest, most revealing form: his drawings. There is no call for esoteric, psychoanalytical divinations of their meanings. They speak for themselves in the realistic, humanized tradition established by Giotto di Båndone and carried on by Dutch and Flemish folk painters, with the spirit of the two Breughels; by James Gillray, Thomas Rowlandson, Francisco Goya y Lucientes, Rodolphe Töpffer, Jean Louis Forain, John Leech, Gustave Dore, George Cruikshank, Honore Daumier, Wilhelm Busch, Eugene Delacroix, Heinrich Kley, Caran d'Ache, George Du Maurier, George Grosz, F. B. Opper, George Belcher, and others in the evolution of genre art that reflects human conduct and environments critically — not in imaginary states of idealism or monsterism.

Comic strips have been an ever flowing fount of fresh vernacular phraseology: "tanks awfully," "you sassy thing," "time's a-wastin'," "heebie-jeebies," "goon," "tank-town," "yard bird," "twerp," "hot dog," "After you, my dear Alphonse," "crepe-hanger," "Dagwood sandwich," "No matter how thin you slice it, it's still boloney," — the latter a classic Goldberg contribution. But Goldberg's is the only name established internationally as a picturesque figure of speech, although "Hogarthian" has had some popular usage as synonym or metaphor.

"Rube Goldbergian" is found repeatedly in files of the august *Congressional Record* at Washington, as an epithet with which lawmakers have labeled each other's projects in "New Deal," "Fair Deal," "Great Society" aspirations. It has been an allusion similarly in legislative bodies of other nations. Usage dictated formal acceptance by dictionary editors.

Thomas Craven, the author of *Men of Art, A Treasury of Art Masterpieces, A Treasury of American Prints,* noted in a monumental study of modern pictorial humor that Goldberg's cartoons of a fictitious Prof. Lucifer Gorgonzola Butts, "in which he complicated the performance of the simplest act by a screwball apparatus, burlesquing the machine age and the wasted energy of the poor boobs who accumulate so much baggage for so short a journey," had done much to set the world straight in its thinking about pretentiously glorious research, inventiveness, industrial design.

Ironically, more than one Goldberg "invention" anticipated actuality. A notable example was his "Portable developing and printing kit." But Goldberg didn't claim this eventuated in the Polaroid type of camera, for his idea went further: his device burned the finished product — "to save your friends the agony of looking at your pictures when you get home."

Goldberg wit embodied in an "invention" frequently has a persuasive logic. Charles F. Kettering, inventor of the first practical automotive self-starter and engineering genius of the General Motors Corporation, was a devotee of Goldberg contrivances. Students in technical schools constructed test models from the Goldberg "blueprints" and found many actually workable, even if useless. The whole series has had a stimulating appeal to engineers for the same reason science-fiction is attractive to scientists.

Goldberg was ahead of hosiery manufacturers with a design for a garterless sock. This was emphasized in conclusions reached by Wilson Curry after examining some 2,000 Goldberg cartoons for the magazine *Mechanix Illustrated*. "Goldberg tries to solve real life problems that get people down, year after year. He deals with social problems . . . the difficulties of eating a buffet supper . . . doing away with hat checking," Mr. Curry wrote.

This is contrary to the motivation Goldberg gives himself. He regards all humorists as rebels and his "inventions" as manifestations of a one-man insurrection against needlessly multifarious gadgetry of the machine age that enslaves man instead of freeing him from nonrewarding labor. Thus *Rube Goldberg vs. The Machine Age* was chosen by the publishers as the most appropriate title for an unique retrospective exhibition of Goldberg's works in book form.

During the preparation of this volume, an-other confirmation of the validity of a Goldberg philosophical tenet was presented. (It is a Goldberg Law — challenging Prof. C. Northcote Parkinson as a natural lawmaker — that the more extremes to which a gadget-maker goes in irrational complexity, the more people will go for it.) News came that a Japanese manufacturer was materializing a Goldberg "invention" as a handy cigarette lighter. While psychoanalysts have been contemplating their navels and concluding the common man is a captive of an Oedipus complex, sales managers of gadget producers have exploited their awareness that the common man actually has a predominant Prometheus complex. Goldberg, most expressive resistant to the machine age, could be confronted with the obsolescence of the simple match's being insured by a gadget he inspired satirically.

One other aspect of the Goldberg inventiveness should be noted. Text with the cartoons tends to be, paradoxically, a distraction from ingenious details of the drawings. Removal of the text, to compel the reader to deduce the operation for himself, induces appreciation of Goldberg's technique with plain pen and ink. He habitually eschewed Ben Day shadings; favored pantomime over "balloons," and avoided onomatopoetic sound — *biff! boom! aarh!* — effects. A perceptive viewer can see in the linear compositions leaving so much to a stimulated imagination, an identity with the later works of Alexander Calder, specifically the latter's mobiles, and the ribald sculpture and paintings of Joan Miro. (The Spaniard, like Goldberg, was trained as an engineer.)

Although Goldberg's name is identified singularly with ridiculous inventions, a dozen or more Goldberg comic strip creations amused and captivated readers over five decades. Extraordinary qualities of Goldberg editorial cartoons, short stories, essays, poetry, song lyrics, and, finally, sculpture are evident in this volume.

Unfortunately, no substantiation is presented herein Goldberg has distinction as a colorist. All his works in this collection, except the sculpture and an exercise in his youth as copyist, were conceived as black and white drawings. Those which appeared on newsprint chromatically, such as the *Boob McNutt* Sunday pages, had red, yellow and blue key plates added in the photoengraving Ben Day process. Artists of the newspaper strips and comic pamphlets have been denied means of having color effects of their choice, such as Hogarth, Goya, Beerbohm, Keppler, Raemakers have in their cartoon and caricature plates. A few surviving *Invention* originals in full color show there could have been remarkable results if the Goldberg creativeness had not been under restraint chromatically in the *Inventions, Boob McNutt,* and other series in the newspapers.

Actual examples of the latter in the limited, poorly selective color of newspaper comic strip printing now are rarities comparable to the comic *tabulae* of the Romans, the gargoyle reliefs of solemn Gothic architecture, the originals of the artists Goldberg identifies in following pages as influential in his beginnings.

There is justification for considering the volume as both a retrospective exhibition and a preserver of important examples of a great artist's work that might otherwise be lost. The Goldberg Collection of the Bancroft Library, University of California (Berkeley), lacks substantial representation of his earlier cartoons. The principal resources for a majority of reproductions of the "primitives" are public libraries. Most libraries have microfilmed their newspaper files and disposed of the originals. Microfilm enlargements do not yield a reproduction as sharply defined as black and white originals, and minimize the qualities of color-pages. Furthermore, the microfilms have a limited durability.

Acknowledgments are due The Bancroft Library of the University of California (Berkeley); The Print Collection, and the Newspaper Division, of the New York Public Library; The New-York Historical Society; the Library of Congress; Mr. C. V. McAdam, McNaught Syndicate; Register & Tribune Syndicate; Cosmopolitan magazine; Good Housekeeping magazine; Curtis Publishing Co. (The Saturday Evening Post); Crowell-Collier Publishing Co. (Collier's Weekly); Doubleday & Co., Inc.; Mills Music Co., Inc.; Mechanix Illustrated magazine; Pageant magazine; Mr. Gilbert Seldes and The New Republic magazine; *A History of American Graphic Humor,* by William Murrell (The Macmillan Co.: 1938); Mr. Thomas Craven; *Comic Art in America,* by Stephen Becker (Simon & Schuster: New York, 1959); *The Funnies: An American Idiom,* edited by Harry Manning White & Robert H. Abel (The Macmillan Co.: New York, 1963); *A History of the Comic Strip,* by Pierre Couperie & Maurice C. Horn (Crown Publishers: New York, 1968); *The Penguin Book of the Comics,* by George Perry & Alan Aldridge (Penguin Books: London and Baltimore, 1967); The Vanguard Press; The John Day Co.; Franklin Watts, Inc.; The Victor Hammer Galleries, New York City; Mr. John Steinbeck. Last, but not least, Mr. Ralph Hollenbeck, the indefatigable researcher who rediscovered many significant early Goldberg works.

CLARK KINNAIRD
New York, July 1968.

1   The Invention of the "Inventions"

I take a little pride in the inventions vicariously ascribed to Professor Lucifer Gorgonzola Butts, a subconscious offspring of my days at University of California. Some things the students had to do in the College of Mining impressed me very forcibly. Especially the course

in analytic mechanics. Frederick Slate, Professor of Physics, directed this course, and it seemed to me that the university had used rare judgment in its choice of the right man for the post. Analytic mechanics and Freddy Slate were exactly suited to each other. In analytic mechanics you were introduced to the funniest-looking contrivances ever conceived by the human mind and in Professor Slate you met a human with a red beard, large Adam's apple, and big goldrimmed spectacles perched on his head. A fine, scholarly gentleman, too. The fellows all loved him.

Professor Slate had devised a machine by which the weight of the earth could be determined. It was a system of tubes, retorts, hoses, and what appeared to be odds and ends.

What knocked me over completely was the name he had given to the crazy-looking contraption. He called it a *Barodik*. Think of anybody calling anything a *Barodik!* You could spend years juggling the letters of the alphabet without getting a name as beautiful as the one Professor Slate had snatched out of thin air for his invention. A *Barodik* could be anything in the world. If I hadn't known what it was and somebody had asked me to guess, I should have snatched an answer out of thin air and said, a surgical contraption used in acute cases of collar-button poisoning. Certainly I should never have suspected that it was an instrument which gave you your choice of answers as to the earth's tonnage. It seemed to me that anything so beautifully named had a much bigger mission in life.

In the course of years thousands of letters have reached me asking how I ever happened to get started on my line of drawing strange-looking inventions designed to perform commonplace but annoying tasks, such as catching a mouse or getting an olive out of a long-necked bottle. Well, the inspiration was Freddy Slate's *Barodik*. He was so serious about it, which had a gorgeous name and was never scientifically wrong — though never actually right, as far as I could see — that I just simply never recovered from the exposure.

In other words, I went *Barodik* in college and couldn't be cured. One of my fondest recollections of college days is when our class of 1904 put on a show and Lambert Coblentz, Doc Bisbee, and I went on as the Three Barodik Brothers. The most delightful part of the whole performance to us was that Professor Slate didn't know until he read the program and saw the title of our act that he had created a masterpiece in nomenclature. But I didn't start to invent my *Barodiks* until about a decade after I left the University. I merely broadened the scope of the *Barodik* by adding mice, rising yeast, toy windmills, midgets and other elements working in a chain reaction to accomplish something trivial.

Every man is a self-appointed missionary of some kind. My pet mission has been to rescue sundry backs from cracking under the strain of carrying inhuman loads. I could never quite understand why sculptors have such an apparent mania for making people hold up heavy objects. I see no logical reason for compelling strong men to support the facade of the municipal building or any excuse for putting a lot of nice, symmetrical young ladies to work as stanchions for the fountain in the town's public square. In fact, it seems to me that the quota of human donkeys in the world is quite sufficient without overexertion. Why on earth should art stress one of the most disagreeable tasks of mankind — that of lugging things around? It would be just as reasonable to memorialize a toothache or an attack of gout.

The impressions of youth are lasting. In childhood I felt deep compassion for the mute serfs of artdom about our home who had nothing more exciting to do than to stand around all day balancing the newel lights, floor lamps, electroliers and other weighty impedimenta. A statue of Atlas appealed especially to my juvenile sympathies. Here was the original hardluck guy. Whenever I felt imposed upon for being required to carry a scuttle of coal up from the cellar, I'd take one look at Atlas and think how lucky he'd regard himself if he had nothing heavier than a scuttle of coal to tote through life. Poor Atlas? In his presence you realize the truth of the old maxim that nothing is ever so bad that it couldn't be worse.

Since those days of daily contact with the misguided statuary and bric-a-brac of our San Francisco home, it has been my ambition to do what I could to emancipate Atlas and his fellow slaves from the state of bondage designed for them by the old masters. Caricatures of sculpture have been the outlet for this philanthropic impulse. If a drawing which shows, let us say, a complicated group of nine gladiators holding up one dinky light achieves its purpose of being grotesquely funny, the big kick I get out of it is not that, but rather the fact that I have been able to give these overworked strong men a good break, in accordance with a resolution reached years ago.

PULL STRING (A) WHICH CAUSES SECONDARY STRING (B) TO MOVE SCISSORS AND CUT ONE HAIR FROM WOODEN HORSE'S TAIL - CLUTCH (E) GRABS HAIR, LIFTS IT AT PULL OF STRING (D) AND DROPS IT IN TUBE (F) - TINCTURE OF IRON DROPS ON HAIR FROM BEAKER (G) - HAIR FALLS INTO HANDS OF TOY-SAILOR (H) WHO TIES A SAILOR'S KNOT ON THE END OF IT - WHEN IT LEAVES SAILOR'S HANDS, FAN (I) BLOWS IT INTO MOUTH OF BALD-HEADED MAN - STRONG ELECTRIC MAGNET (J) PULLS IRON-SOAKED HAIR THROUGH THE TOP OF HIS HEAD - SAILOR'S KNOT PREVENTS IT FROM LEAVING HEAD - OPERATION IS REPEATED UNTIL THERE IS ENOUGH HAIR ON TOP OF HEAD TO COMB.

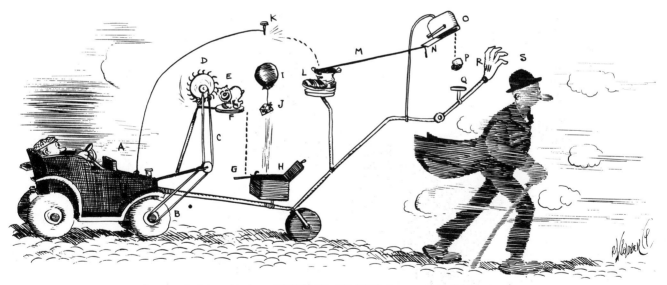

BUY AUTOMOBILE (A) FOR $275 AND HIRE CHAUFFEUR TO DRIVE IN BACK OF YOU ON WINDY DAY - MOTION OF BELT (B), ATTACHED TO FRONT WHEEL, IS COMMUNICATED TO BELT (C) WHICH TURNS TICKLER (D) - PICKLE-SPANIEL (E) LAUGHS UNTIL HE CHOKES AND FALLS OFF PLATFORM (F) HITTING CATCH (G) AND OPENING BOX (H) - BALLOON (I), WITH SUSPENDED PIECE OF CHEESE (J) RISES AND BURSTS ON PIN (K) - CHEESE DROPS INTO SHOE (L) - STRENGTH OF CHEESE CAUSES SHOE TO WALK AWAY PULLING SHOE-LACE (M) AND SLIDING COVER (N) OFF BOX (O) RELEASING TEN-POUND BISCUIT (P) - BISCUIT HITS SURFACE (Q)' CAUSING ARM HOLDING IRON HAND (R) TO COME DOWN WITH A JOLT, AND HAND PRESSES HAT (S) ON HEAD SO TIGHT IT HAS TO BE BLASTED OFF WITH DYNAMITE UPON YOUR RETURN HOME.

BE YOUR OWN DENTIST !

FIRST TIE YOURSELF SECURELY TO CHAIR (A) AND WIGGLE FOOT (B). FEATHER (C) TICKLES BIRD (D)- AS BIRD SHAKES WITH LAUGHTER, IT MIXES COCKTAIL IN SHAKER (E)- BIRD FALLS FORWARD, SPILLING COCKTAIL, AND SQUIRREL (F) GETS SOUSED - IN HIS DRUNKEN EXCITEMENT, SQUIRREL REVOLVES CAGE (G), WHICH TURNS CRANK (H) AND PLAYS PHONOGRAPH RECORD (I)- SONG (J) GETS DWARF (K) HOT UNDER COLLAR AND FLAMES (L) IGNITE FUSE (M) WHICH SETS OFF CANNON (N), SHOOTING OUT CANNON BALL (O), CAUSING STRING (P) TO PULL TOOTH !

A LABOR-SAVING NEW YEAR'S EVE NOISE-MAKER.

YOU CAN GET ALL THE NOISE YOU WANT OUT OF A TRAMP AND A BOWL OF SOUP.

MAKING IT EASY FOR THE MAN WHO BLOWS THE HORN.

A DISH-WASHER CAN MIX BUSINESS WITH PLEASURE NEW YEAR'S EVE.

Go to ball grounds and stand near fence (A) - during game, ball (B) is knocked over fence and hits dog (C) pushing him to ground - string (D), tied to dog's tail, pulls cork (E) from champagne bottle (F) - sound of wine being opened causes waiter (G) to expect big tip and he extends right hand in receptive position - it starts to rain. Rain falls in waiter's hand and runs in steady stream into pipe (H) - water finally drops on blade of grass (I) - grass grows until it tickles soft-shell crab (J) under the chin, making him laugh - he falls to platform (L), moving spring (M) downward and pulling string (N) which opens box (O) and releases firefly (P) - firefly, thinking picture of candle (Q) is real thing, gets jealous and springs upon it, passing cigar (R) and giving it required light.

When you find you've lost your collar button again, you wave arms in anger - fist (A) presses bulb (B) and squirts water (C) into eye of yiffik bird (D) - bird is temporarily blinded & walks off perch (E), falling into car (F) of scenic railway (G) - car descends, causing cord (H) to tilt bar (I) - wooden finger (J) presses referee doll (K) making it say "play ball" - pitcher (L) of midget giants grabs ball (M) which is attached to handle of phonograph (N) and winds up - phonograph record asks, "where is at?" - philosopher father (O) of pitcher, who is even smaller than his son, is puzzled over question and walks around trying to figure it out - he is so absorbed in problem, he walks under bureau (P) and bumps into collar button (Q), yelling "ouch" and showing you where collar button is.

WHEN YOU SAY "HAVE A DRINK", NATURAL MOTION OF HAND (A) PULLS STRING (B) AND LIFTS LID (C), RELEASING VODKA FUMES (D) WHICH MAKE RUSSIAN DANCING-BUG (E) FEEL GIDDY - HE STARTS DANCING NATIONL DANCE OF RUSSIA AND REVOLVES PLATFORM (F) - PULLEY (G) TURNS CORKSCREW (H) AND IT SINKS INTO CORK (I) BRINGING DOWN DISC (J) WHICH HITS SURFACE (K) AND CAUSES WOODEN HAND TO PUSH IRON BALL (M) OFF SUPPORT (N), CAUSING CORD (O) TO PULL CORKSCREW WITH CORK FROM BOTTLE.

AT LAST! THE GREAT BRAIN OF THE DISTINGUISHED MAN OF SCIENCE GIVES THE WORLD THE SIMPLE AUTOMATIC SHEET MUSIC TURNER!

PRESS LEFT FOOT (A) ON PEDAL (B) WHICH PULLS DOWN HANDLE (C) ON TIRE PUMP (D). PRESSURE OF AIR BLOWS WHISTLE (E). GOLD FISH (F) BELIEVES THIS IS DINNER SIGNAL AND STARTS FEEDING ON WORM (G). THE PULL ON STRING (H) RELEASES BRACE (I), DROPPING SHELF (J), LEAVING WEIGHT (K) WITHOUT SUPPORT. NATURALLY, HATRACK (L) IS SUDDENLY EXTENDED AND BOXING GLOVE (M) HITS PUNCHING BAG (N) WHICH, IN TURN, IS PUNCTURED BY SPIKE (O).

ESCAPING AIR BLOWS AGAINST SAIL (P) WHICH IS ATTACHED TO PAGE OF MUSIC (Q), WHICH TURNS GENTLY AND MAKES WAY FOR THE NEXT OUTBURST OF SWEET OR SOUR MELODY.

AFTER TRYING UNSUCCESSFULLY TO OPEN WINDOW FOR HALF AN HOUR, YOU RELIEVE YOUR ANGER BY CHOKING PARROT(A) - DOG (B) HEARS PARROT'S GROANS AND WEEPS OUT OF SYMPATHY-TEARS(C) SOAK SPONGE (D), CAUSING ITS WEIGHT TO PULL STRING (E) WHICH LIFTS TOP OFF CAGE (F) AND RELEASES WOODPECKER (G)- WOODPECKER CHEWS AWAY SHELF(H) AND HEAVY BISCUIT (I) FALLS ON BROOM-HANDLE (J), CAUSING IT TO ACT AS LEVER IN RAISING WINDOW - AFTER REPEATING THIS OPERATION SIX TIMES WITHOUT SUCCESS, TAKE HAMMER (K) AND BREAK GLASS IN WINDOW, ALLOWING FRESH AIR TO ENTER ROOM.

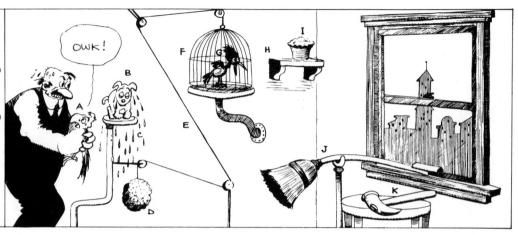

ELEPHANT (A) EATS PEANUTS (B) - AS BAG GETS LIGHTER WEIGHT (C) DROPS AND SPIKE (D) PUNCTURES BALLOON (E) - EXPLOSION SCARES MONKEY (F) - HIS HAT(G) FLIES OFF AND RELEASES HOOK (H), CAUSING SPRING(I) TO PULL STRING (J), WHICH TILTS TENNIS RACKET(K)-RACKET HITS BALL (L), MAKING IT SPIN AROUND ON ATTACHED STRING, THEREBY SCREWING CORKSCREW INTO CORK (M) - BALL HITS SLEEPING DOG (N) WHO JUMPS AND PULLS CORK OUT OF BOTTLE WITH STRING (O) - MY, HOW SIMPLE!

MAN IN BATH TUB SNAPS FINGERS AND PET GOLF-BEAKED SOAP-HAWK (A) HITS SOAP(B) INTO BASEBALL GLOVE (C) - REBOUND OF SPRING(D) CAUSES GLOVE TO THROW SOAP PAST CAT (E) INTO TROUGH (F) - BREEZE FROM FLYING SOAP CAUSES CAT TO CATCH COLD - SHE SNEEZES, BLOWING SOAP OFF TROUGH-SOAP HITS STRING (G), WHICH PULLS TRIGGER OF PISTOL (H), SHOOTING RAM(I) AGAINST SMALL CAR (J), INTO WHICH SOAP HAS MEANTIME FALLEN- CAR CARRIES SOAP UP PLATFORM (K), DUMPING IT BACK INTO TUB AND MAN CAN CONTINUE WITH HIS BATH.

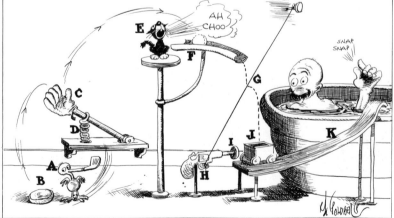

WEIGHT OF CIGARETTE BUTT
LOWERS ASH-STAND AND
CAUSES POINT (A) TO RISE
AND PUNCTURE BALLOON (B)-
POLICEMAN (C), HEARING REPORT
LIKE GUN, OPENS WINDOW (D),
WHICH PULLS STRING (E) AND
TURNS ON GAS STOVE (F) AND
STARTS ONIONS AND GARLIC
COOKING - PARROT (G) IS
SOON GASSED AND FALLS TO
PLATFORM (H), CAUSING TIN
CAN (I) TO FLY UP IN AIR
PAST GOAT (J) AND OUT OF HIS
REACH - THIS CAUSES GOAT
KEEN DISAPPOINTMENT
AND HE CRIES BITTERLY-
TEARS (K) FALL ON
CIGARETTE BUTT AND EX-
TINGUISH IT COMPLETELY.

WAIT FOR RAINSTORM - RAIN (A)
WATERS PLANT (B) WHICH GROWS
AND PUSHES END OF PADDLE (C)
CAUSING OTHER END (D) TO PRESS
BICYCLE PUMP (E) AND BLOW UP
TOY BALLOON (F) WHICH MAKES
NOISE (G) LIKE CRYING BABY-
PET CRANBERRY-SPANIEL (H),
THINKING BABY IS IN TROUBLE,
JUMPS AND PULLS STRING (I)
WHICH PULLS CORK (J) CAUSING
CARBOLIC ACID IN BOTTLE (K) TO
SET BEETLE (L) ON FIRE-BEETLE
RUNS UP TROUGH (M) AND IGNITES
FUSE (N), SETTING OFF SKY-
ROCKET (O) WHICH PULLS PAR-
TITION (P) FROM CENTER OF
CAGE (Q) AND GIVES MOTHS
ACCESS TO HAIR-LOOK IN
MIRROR (R) - WHEN MOTHS
HAVE EATEN OFF ENOUGH HAIR
DROWN THEM WITH GLASS OF
WATER (S).

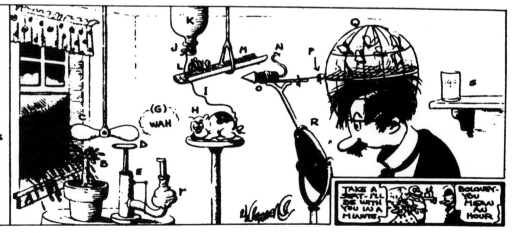

GET ONE OF OUR PATENT FANS AND KEEP COOL

Take hold of handles (A) of wheelbarrow (B) and start walking- pulley (C) turns kicking arrangement (D) which annoys bear (E) - bear suspects doll (F) and eats it, pulling string (G) which starts mechanical bird (H) saying, "do you love me?"- love-bird (I) keeps shaking head "yes", causing fan (J) to move back and forth making nice breeze blow right in your face.

Flame from lamp (A) catches on curtain (B) and fire department sends stream of water (C) through window- dwarf (D) thinks it is raining and reaches for umbrella (E), pulling string (F) and lifting end of platform (G) - iron ball (H) falls and pulls string (I), causing hammer (J) to hit plate of glass (K) - crash of glass wakes up pup (L) and mother dog (M) rocks him to sleep in cradle (N), causing attached wooden hand (O) to move up and down along your back.

POOR FELLOW, HE'S TAKING AN AWFUL BEATING

BOLONEY! FOR THE MONEY HE'S GETTING I'D TAKE ONE, TOO

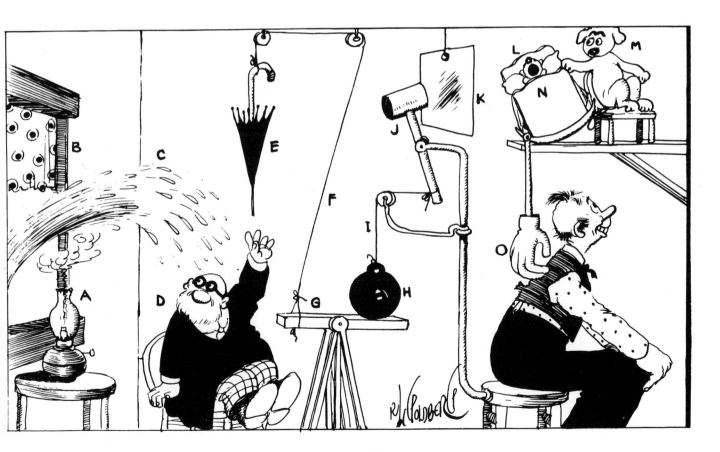

The Inventions of Professor Lucifer G. Butts, A.K.

PROFESSOR BUTTS IS HIT ON THE HEAD BY A METEOR AND WHEN THE AUTHORITIES GO THROUGH HIS POCKETS TO IDENTIFY HIM ALL THEY FIND IS A DIAGRAM SHOWING HOW TO KEEP AWAKE DURING BUSINESS HOURS.

AS OFFICE BOY OPENS DOOR(A) IT CAUSES CORD(B) TO SLACKEN AND LOWER CALENDAR(C) MARKED **MONDAY.** CHINESE LAUNDRYMAN(D), SEEING CALENDAR, IMMEDIATELY KNOWS IT'S WASH DAY AND STARTS WASHING SHIRTS. MOTION OF CHINAMAN'S ARM CAUSES FILE(E) TO RUB AGAINST CHAIN(F) CUTTING IT IN HALF AND RELEASING TRAINED MONKEY(G). MONKEY REMEMBERING HIS EARLY DAYS AS A CIRCUS JOCKEY JUMPS ON HOBBY HORSE(H) AND STARTS ROCKING, CAUSING BELLOWS(I) TO PUMP AIR THROUGH TUBE(J). AIR BLOWS CAPTIVE MOSQUITO(K) AGAINST YOUR NECK WHICH BITES YOU BACK TO WAKEFULNESS. IF THE CHINAMAN ASKS FOR PAY FOR DOING THE LAUNDRY, GIVE HIM A CHECK ON YOUR WIFE'S BANK.

PROFESSOR BUTTS STANDS IN FRONT OF AN X-RAY AND SEES AN IDEA INSIDE HIS HEAD SHOWING HOW TO KEEP SHOP WINDOWS CLEAN.

PASSING MAN(A) SLIPS ON BANANA PEEL(B) CAUSING HIM TO FALL ON RAKE(C) AS HANDLE OF RAKE RISES IT THROWS HORSESHOE(D) ONTO ROPE(E) WHICH SAGS, THEREBY TILTING SPRINKLING CAN(F). WATER(G) SATURATES MOP(H). PICKLE TERRIER(I) THINKS IT IS RAINING, GETS UP TO RUN INTO HOUSE AND UPSETS SIGN(J) THROWING IT AGAINST NON-TIPPING CIGAR ASH RECEIVER(K) WHICH CAUSES IT TO SWING BACK AND FORTH AND SWISH THE MOP AGAINST WINDOW PANE, WIPING IT CLEAN.

IF MAN BREAKS HIS NECK BY FALL MOVE AWAY BEFORE COP ARRIVES.

PROFESSOR BUTTS STEPS INTO AN OPEN ELEVATOR SHAFT AND WHEN HE LANDS AT THE BOTTOM HE FINDS A SIMPLE ORANGE SQUEEZING MACHINE. MILK MAN TAKES EMPTY MILK BOTTLE (A) PULLING STRING (B) WHICH CAUSES SWORD (C) TO SEVER CORD (D) AND ALLOW GUILLOTINE BLADE (E) TO DROP AND CUT ROPE (F) WHICH RELEASES BATTERING RAM (G). RAM BUMPS AGAINST OPEN DOOR (H) CAUSING IT TO CLOSE. GRASS SICKLE (I) CUTS A SLICE OFF END OF ORANGE (J) AT THE SAME TIME SPIKE (K) STABS "PRUNE HAWK (L) HE OPENS HIS MOUTH TO YELL IN AGONY, THEREBY RELEASING PRUNE AND ALLOWING DIVER'S BOOT (M) TO DROP AND STEP ON SLEEPING OCTOPUS (N). OCTOPUS AWAKENS IN A RAGE AND SEEING DIVER'S FACE WHICH IS PAINTED ON ORANGE, ATTACKS IT AND CRUSHES IT WITH TENTACLES, THEREBY CAUSING ALL THE JUICE IN THE ORANGE TO RUN INTO GLASS (O).
LATER ON YOU CAN USE THE LOG TO BUILD A LOG CABIN WHERE YOU CAN RAISE YOUR SON TO BE PRESIDENT LIKE ABRAHAM LINCOLN.

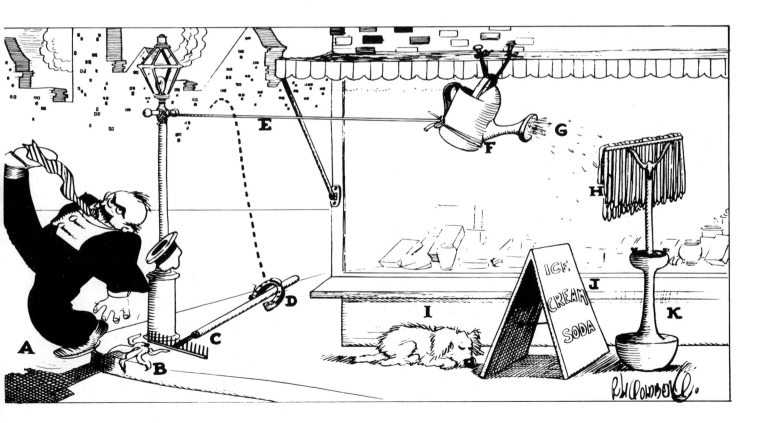

PROFESSOR BUTTS WALKS THROUGH A GLASS DOOR AND WHEN THEY PICK OUT THE PIECES THEY FIND AN IDEA FOR AN AUTOMATIC CIGAR CUTTER. ZOOVLE-PUP (A) SEEING MASTER COMING UP THE PATH WAGS TAIL FOR JOY UPSETTING CANDLE (B) WHICH SETS FIRE TO EXCELSIOR (C) IN BOX ON FLOOR. FLAMES (D) HEAT POP CORN (E) WHICH ESKIMO MISTAKES FOR FALLING SNOW AND DANCES WITH GLEE, GETTING HIS BELT (F) CAUGHT ON SUSPENDED HOOK (G), WHICH JERKS STRING (H) AND PULLS TRIGGER OF PISTOL (I). BULLET (J) HITS ZINGUS BIRD WHICH OPENS ITS MOUTH IN SURPRISE AND DROPS WORM (K). SWORDFISH (L) JUMPS OUT OF BOWL (M) AFTER WORM AND ITS SWORD NEATLY LOPS OFF END OF CIGAR (N).

NOW, THE BIG IDEA IS TO GET THE SWORD-FISH BACK INTO THE BOWL. I WOULD SUGGEST THAT YOU LEAVE THAT ENTIRE-LY TO THE SWORDFISH.

PROFESSOR BUTTS, WHILE OVERHAULING A 1907 FORD, FINDS AN IDEA FOR A SIMPLE WAY TO SHARPEN ICE SKATES.
WIRE BUNDLE-BASKET (A) IN SPORTING STORE HITS FLOOR-WALKER (B) AND KNOCKS HIM DIZZY. AS HE SINKS TO FLOOR HIS KNEES HIT END OF SEE-SAW (C) WHICH TOSSES BASKET BALL (D) INTO BROKEN NET (E). BALL FALLS ON TENNIS RACKET (F) CAUSING GROUP OF TIN CANS (G) TO FLY UP OUT OF REACH OF HUNGRY GOAT (H). GOAT, BEING ROBBED OF HIS DINNER, JUMPS IN FURY AND BUTTS HIS HEAD AGAINST BOXING DUMMY (I). DUMMY SWAYS BACK AND FORTH ON SWIVEL BASE (J), CAUSING TWO ECCENTRIC WHEELS (K) TO PUSH FILE (L) ACROSS BLADE OF SKATE (M) AND MAKE IT SHARP ENOUGH TO USE FOR SKATING IN THE WINTER AND SHAVING IN THE SUMMER.
YOU MAY THINK IT CRUEL TO HIT THE FLOOR-WALKER ON THE HEAD. BUT WE ASSURE YOU THERE IS NOTHING INSIDE WHICH CAN BE DAMAGED.

Professor Butts, training for the Olymic Games, broad jumps into the Grand Ganyon by mistake and, before he reaches bottom, has plenty of time to invent a neat little fire extinguisher.

Porter (A) smells smoke coming from room and in the excitement sticks his head through window screen to investigate. Little boy remembering carnival, throws baseball (B) which bounces off porter's head and breaks glass in aquarium (C), causing water to run into trough (D) and revolve paddle wheel (E) which winds rope (F), pulling knife (G) and cutting cord (H). Shoe (I) falls on baby's face, baby sheds copious tears. Splashing of tears makes bull frog (J) think of babbling brook and he starts swimming causing file (K) to cut chain (L) which breaks and allows trees (M) to snap upright and pull wet blanket (N) over burning waste basket, thereby extinguishing fire.

If the fire doesn't happen to be in the waste basket, call out the fire department.

PROFESSOR BUTTS GETS HIS WHISKERS CAUGHT IN A LAUNDRY WRINGER AND AS HE COMES OUT THE OTHER END HE THINKS OF AN IDEA FOR A SIMPLE PARACHUTE. AS AVIATOR JUMPS FROM PLANE FORCE OF WIND OPENS UMBRELLA (A) WHICH PULLS CORD (B) AND CLOSES SHEARS (C), CUTTING OFF CORNER OF FEATHER PILLOW (D). AS WHITE FEATHERS (E) FLY FROM PILLOW, PENGUIN (F) MISTAKES THEM FOR SNOW FLAKES AND FLAPS HIS WINGS FOR JOY WHICH DRAWS BUCK-SAW (G) BACK AND FORTH CUTTING LOG OF WOOD (H). AS PIECE OF WOOD FALLS INTO BASKET (I) ITS WEIGHT CAUSES ROPE (J) TO PULL TRIGGER OF GUN (K) WHICH EXPLODES AND SHOOTS LOCK FROM CAGE (L) RELEASING GIANT UMPHA BIRD (M) WHICH FLIES AND KEEPS AVIATOR AFLOAT WITH ROPE (N). AVIATOR BREAKS PAPER BAG OF CORN (O) CAUSING CORN TO FALL TO GROUND. WHEN BIRD SWOOPS DOWN TO EAT CORN, FLIER, UNHOOKS APPARATUS AND WALKS HOME.
THE BIGGEST PROBLEM IS WHERE TO GET THE UMPHA BIRD. WRITE YOUR CONGRESSMAN.

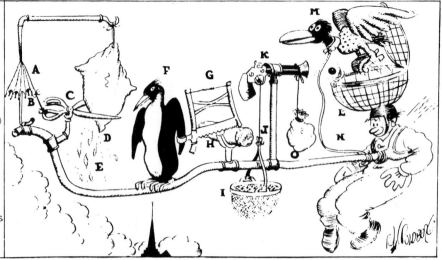

PROFESSOR BUTTS FLIES THROUGH THE WIND-SHIELD OF HIS CAR AND WHEN THEY PICK OUT THE BROKEN GLASS THEY FIND AN IDEA FOR A SELF-ROLLING RUG.
PLACE FRESH PIE (A) ON WINDOW SILL (B) TO COOL. WHEN TRAMP (C) SNEAKS UP TO STEAL IT, HOUSE-MAID (D) FALLS BACK WITH FRIGHT INTO ROCK-ING CHAIR (E) WHICH TILTS PEDESTAL (F), CAUS-ING MARBLE STATUE OF DIVING VENUS (G) TO DIVE INTO GOLDFISH BOWL (H) AND SPLASH WATER ON PLANT (I) WHICH GROWS AND TURNS ON SWITCH (J) OF RADIO (K) WHICH PLAYS OLD TUNE CALLED "OCEANA ROLL". LITTLE TRICK ROLLING CIRCUS ELEPHANT (L), HEARING TUNE, DOES HIS STUFF AND KEEPS ROLLING OVER AND OVER UNTIL RUG (M) IS COMPLETELY WRAPPED AROUND HIM AND FLOOR IS CLEARED FOR DANCING.
RUG WRAPPED AROUND DELICATE LITTLE ELEPHANT ALSO KEEPS HIM FROM CATCHING COLD FROM DRAFT COMING THROUGH OPEN WINDOW.

PROFESSOR BUTTS TRIES TO FIX A LEAK IN THE BOILER AND WHEN HE IS RESCUED FROM DROWNING HE COUGHS UP AN IDEA FOR AN OUTBOARD MOTOR THAT REQUIRES NO FUEL.
AS YOU REACH FOR ANCHOR, BUTTON(A) SNAPS LOOSE AND HITS SPIGOT(B) CAUSING BEER TO RUN INTO PAIL(C). WEIGHT PULLS CORD(D) FIRING SHOT GUN(E). REPORT FRIGHTENS SEA GULL(F) WHICH FLIES AWAY AND CAUSES ICE(G) TO LOWER IN FRONT OF FALSE TEETH(H). AS TEETH CHATTER FROM COLD THEY BITE CORD(I) IN HALF ALLOWING POINTED TOOL(J) TO DROP AND RIP BAG OF CORN(K). CORN FALLS INTO NET(L). WEIGHT CAUSES IT TO SNAP LATCH OPENING FLOOR OF CAGE(M) AND DROPPING DUCK INTO SHAFTS(N). AS DUCK(O) TRIES TO REACH CORN IT SWIMS AND CAUSES CANOE TO MOVE AHEAD.
IF THE FALSE TEETH KEEP ON CHATTERING YOU CAN LET THEM CHEW YOUR GUM TO GIVE YOUR OWN JAWS A REST.

GREATEST BRIDGE PROBLEM SOLVED! PROFESSOR BUTTS SHOWS HOW TO SIGNAL YOUR PARTNER WHEN IT IS TIME TO LEAD SPADES.
THROUGH HOLE IN FLOOR(A) DROP LIGHTED CIGARETTE(B) WHICH SETS FIRE TO EXCELSIOR(C). FLAME(D) MAKES GLOW WHICH ROOSTER(E) MISTAKES FOR DAWN. HE CROWS AND JUMPS FROM ROOST(F) LANDING ON HAT-RACK(G) WHICH EXPANDS AND PUSHES LEVER(H) CAUSING SWITCH(I) TO HEAT ELECTRIC PAD(J) AND HATCH EGGS(K). YOUNG CHICKS SAY "PEEP, PEEP." SENTIMENTAL SPANIEL(L) IS TOUCHED BY CUTE SIGHT AND WAGS TAIL WITH DELIGHT, MOVING STICK(M), CAUSING MATCH(N) TO STRIKE ON BOX(O), AND LIGHT FUSE(P). ROCKET(Q) MOVES FORWARD PULLING STRING(R) BRINGING MALLET(S) DOWN ON PARTNER'S FOOT AND GIVING HIM THE REQUIRED SIGNAL. BEFORE STARTING THE GAME BE SURE YOUR CORNS ARE NOT TENDER.

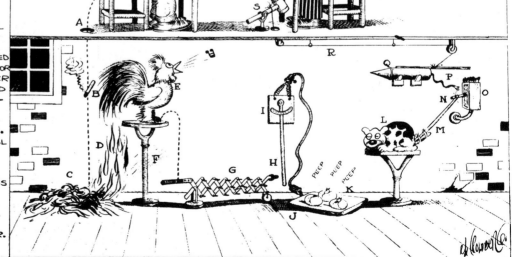

Electric indicator (A) is connected with ticker in stock broker's office and registers price of stock you own – when arm (B) drops to zero, showing you have been wiped out, it hits weight (C) and causes lever (D) to lift imitation nut (E) which is really made of ivory – squirrel (F) jumps with pain when it's teeth bite into ivory nut, causing string (G) to lift lid (H) of pot (I), liberating fumes of hot chowder (J) – clam (K) dives into chowder, pulling cord (L), which simultaneously shoots pistol (M) and empties bottle of poison (N) into glass (O) – if pistol shot does not end your worries, drink poison – if you're still alive after that you're tough enough to go back into the stock market.

Professor Butts gets his think-tank working and evolves the simplified pencil-sharpener.

Open window (A) and fly kite (B). String (C) lifts small door (D) allowing moths (E) to escape and eat red flannel shirt (F). As weight of shirt becomes less, shoe (G) steps on switch (H) which heats electric iron (I) and burns hole in pants (J). Smoke (K) enters hole in tree (L) smoking out opossum (M) which jumps into basket (N) pulling rope (O) and lifting cage (P), allowing woodpecker (Q) to chew wood from pencil (R) exposing lead. Emergency knife (S) is always handy in case opossum or the woodpecker gets sick and can't work.

18

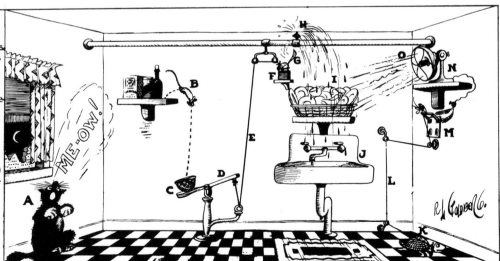

THE PROFESSOR TURNS ON HIS THINK-FAUCET AND DOPES OUT A MACHINE FOR WASHING DISHES WHILE YOU ARE AT THE MOVIES.

WHEN SPOILED TOMCAT(A)DISCOVERS HE IS ALONE HE LETS OUT A YELL WHICH SCARES MOUSE(B)INTO JUMPING INTO BASKET(C), CAUSING LEVER END(D) TO RISE AND PULL STRING(E) WHICH SNAPS AUTOMATIC CIGAR LIGHTER(F). FLAME(G) STARTS FIRE SPRINKLER(H). WATER RUNS ON DISHES (I)AND DRIPS INTO SINK(J). TURTLE(K), THINKING HE HEARS BABBLING BROOK BABBLING, AND HAVING NO SENSE OF DIRECTION, STARTS WRONG WAY AND PULLS STRING(L),WHICH TURNS ON SWITCH (M)THAT STARTS ELECTRIC GLOW HEATER (N). HEAT RAY(O) DRIES THE DISHES.

IF THE CAT AND THE TURTLE GET ON TO YOUR SCHEME AND REFUSE TO COOPERATE, SIMPLY PUT THE DISHES ON THE FRONT PORCH AND PRAY FOR RAIN.

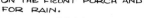

19

20

THE PROFESSOR EMERGES FROM THE GOOFY BOOTH WITH A DEVICE FOR THE EXTERMINATION OF MOTHS.

START SINGING. LADY UPSTAIRS, WHEN SUFFICIENTLY ANNOYED, THROWS FLOWER POT (A) THROUGH AWNING (B). HOLE (C) ALLOWS SUN TO COME THROUGH AND MELT CAKE OF ICE (D). WATER DRIPS INTO PAN (E) RUNNING THROUGH PIPE (F) INTO PAIL (G). WEIGHT OF PAIL CAUSES CORD (H) TO RELEASE HOOK (I) AND ALLOW ARROW (J) TO SHOOT INTO TIRE (K). ESCAPING AIR BLOWS AGAINST TOY SAILBOAT (L) DRIVING IT AGAINST LEVER (M) AND CAUSING BALL TO ROLL INTO SPOON (N) AND PULL STRING (O) WHICH SETS OFF MACHINE GUN (P) DISCHARGING CAMPHOR BALLS (Q). REPORT OF GUN FRIGHTENS LAMB (R) WHICH RUNS AND PULLS CORD (S), OPENING CLOSET DOOR (T). AS MOTHS (U) FLY OUT TO EAT WOOL FROM LAMB'S BACK THEY ARE KILLED BY THE BARRAGE OF MOTH BALLS.

IF ANY OF THE MOTHS ESCAPE AND THERE IS DANGER OF THEIR RETURNING, YOU CAN FOOL THEM BY MOVING.

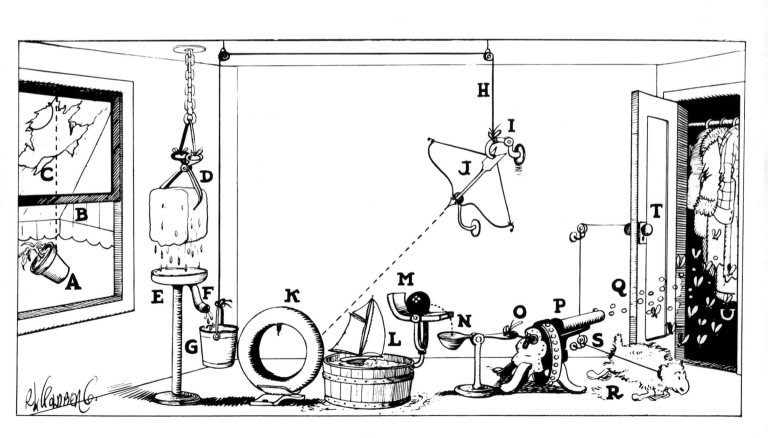

PROFESSOR BUTTS CHOKES ON A PRUNE
PIT AND COUGHS UP AN IDEA FOR AN
AUTOMATIC TYPEWRITER ERASER.
RING FOR OFFICE BOY (A), WHO COMES
RUNNING IN AND STUMBLES OVER FEET
OF WINDOW CLEANER (B). HE GRABS FOR
HAT-RACK (C) TO SAVE HIMSELF. HAT-RACK
FALLS AGAINST BOOKS (D) WHICH DROP ON
RULER (E), CAUSING PEN (F) TO FLY UP AND
PUNCTURE BALLOON (G) WHICH EXPLODES
WITH A LOUD REPORT.
TRAINED MONKEY (H) MISTAKES REPORT FOR
GUN THAT IS THE SIGNAL TO BEGIN HIS
VAUDEVILLE ACT AND HE STARTS
PEDALLING LIKE MAD. THE RUBBER TIRE (I)
PASSES OVER PAPER (J) AND ERASES MIS-
TAKE MADE BY SLEEPY STENOGRAPHER
WHO IS TOO TIRED TO DO IT HERSELF BE-
CAUSE SHE HAD SUCH A LONG WALK HOME
FROM AN AUTOMOBILE RIDE THE NIGHT
BEFORE.
IT IS ADVISABLE TO HAVE YOUR OFFICE
OVER A GARAGE SO YOU CAN GET QUICK
SERVICE IN CASE OF A PUNCTURE.

PROFESSOR BUTTS FALLS ON HIS HEAD
AND DOPES OUT A SIMPLIFIED CAN-
OPENER WHILE HE IS STILL GROGGY.
GO OUTSIDE AND CALL UP YOUR HOME. WHEN
PHONE BELL RINGS, MAID (A) MISTAKES IT FOR
AN ALARM CLOCK - SHE AWAKENS AND
STRETCHES, PULLING CORD (B) WHICH RAISES
END OF LADLE (C). BALL (D) DROPS INTO NET (E)
CAUSING GOLF CLUB (F) TO SWING AGAINST
BALL (G), MAKING A CLEAN DRIVE AND UP-
SETTING MILK CAN (H). MILK SPILLS INTO GLASS
(I) AND THE WEIGHT PULLS SWITCH ON RADIO
(J). WALTZING MICE (K) HEARING MUSIC AND
PROCEED TO DANCE, CAUSING REVOLVING
APPARATUS (L) TO SPIN AND TURN. SPIKES (M)
SCRATCH TAIL OF PET DRAGON (N) WHO IN
ANGER EMITS FIRE IGNITING ACETYLENE
TORCH (O) AND BURNING OFF TOP OF
TOMATO CAN (P) AS IT ROTATES.
WHEN NOT OPENING CANS, THE DRAGON
CAN ALWAYS BE KEPT BUSY CHASING
AWAY INCOME TAX INVESTIGATORS
AND PROHIBITION OFFICERS.

PROFESSOR BUTTS MAKES A PARACHUTE JUMP, FORGETS TO PULL THE STRING AND WAKES UP THREE WEEKS LATER WITH AN AUTOMATIC DEVICE FOR KEEPING SCREEN DOORS CLOSED.

HOUSEFLIES(A) SEEING OPEN DOOR, FLY ON PORCH. SPIDER(B) DESCENDS TO CATCH THEM AND FRIGHTENS POTATO-BUG(C) WHICH JUMPS FROM HAMMER(D) ALLOWING IT TO DROP ON PANCAKE TURNER(E) WHICH TOSSES PANCAKE INTO PAN(F). WEIGHT OF PANCAKE CAUSES PAN TO TILT AND PULL CORD WHICH STARTS MECHANICAL SOLDIER(H) WALKING. SOLDIER WALKS TO EDGE OF TABLE AND CATCHES HIS HEAD IN NOOSE(I) THEREBY HANGING HIMSELF. WEIGHT IN NOOSE CAUSES STRING TO PULL LEVER AND PUSH SHOE AGAINST BOWLING BALL(J), THROWING IT INTO HANDS OF CIRCUS MONKEY(K) WHO IS EXPERT BOWLER. MONKEY THROWS BALL AT BOWLING PINS PAINTED ON SCREEN DOOR THEREBY CLOSING IT WITH A BANG.

THE MONKEY IS LIABLE TO GET SORE WHEN HE DISCOVERS THAT THE BOWLING PINS ARE PHONEY SO IT IS A GOOD IDEA TO TAKE HIM TO A REAL BOWLING ALLEY ONCE IN A WHILE JUST TO KEEP HIS GOOD WILL.

A BARBER PUTS A SCALDING TOWEL ON PROFESSOR BUTTS'S FACE AND WHILE HE IS SCREAMING WITH PAIN HE THINKS UP AN INVENTION FOR DIGGING UP BAIT FOR FISHING. THE MAID(A) PEELS AN ONION AND CRIES INTO FUNNEL(B). TEARS(C) RUN THROUGH PIPE(D) AND DRIP INTO PAN(E) OF JEWELER'S SCALE(F), CAUSING END OF BAR(G) TO PRESS AGAINST SMALL BELLOWS(H), WHICH BLOWS INSECT POWDER(I) ON SHELF AND KNOCKS OFF ROACHES(J). ROACHES FALL ON EDGE OF ANTIQUE FAN(K), CAUSING IT TO CLOSE AND EXPOSE SURFACE OF MIRROR(L). SELFISH PALOOKA HOUND(M) SEES HIS REFLECTION IN MIRROR AND, THINKING IT IS ANOTHER DOG, HASTENS TO BURY BONE(N). AS HE DIGS, HE UNCOVERS WORM(O) WHICH IS SEEN IMMEDIATELY BY EARLY BIRD(P) WHO DIVES FOR IT OFF PERCH. WEIGHT(Q) DROPS ON HEAD OF BIRD AND KNOCKS HIM COLD JUST AS HE PULLS WORM FAR ENOUGH OUT OF GROUND FOR FISHERMAN TO GRAB IT EASILY.

WHEN THE EARLY BIRD WAKES UP YOU CAN LET HIM EAT THE ONION JUST SO HE WILL NOT BE GETTING TOO RAW A DEAL.

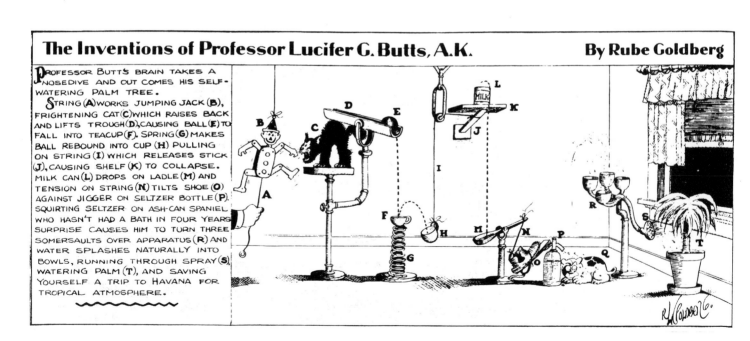

The Inventions of Professor Lucifer G. Butts, A.K.

By Rube Goldberg

PROFESSOR BUTT'S BRAIN TAKES A
NOSEDIVE AND OUT COMES HIS SELF-
WATERING PALM TREE.
STRING (A) WORKS JUMPING JACK (B),
FRIGHTENING CAT (C) WHICH RAISES BACK
AND LIFTS TROUGH (D), CAUSING BALL (E) TO
FALL INTO TEACUP (F). SPRING (G) MAKES
BALL REBOUND INTO CUP (H) PULLING
ON STRING (I) WHICH RELEASES STICK
(J), CAUSING SHELF (K) TO COLLAPSE.
MILK CAN (L) DROPS ON LADLE (M) AND
TENSION ON STRING (N) TILTS SHOE (O)
AGAINST JIGGER ON SELTZER BOTTLE (P).
SQUIRTING SELTZER ON ASH-CAN SPANIEL
WHO HASN'T HAD A BATH IN FOUR YEARS
SURPRISE CAUSES HIM TO TURN THREE
SOMERSAULTS OVER APPARATUS (R) AND
WATER SPLASHES NATURALLY INTO
BOWLS, RUNNING THROUGH SPRAY (S)
WATERING PALM (T), AND SAVING
YOURSELF A TRIP TO HAVANA FOR
TROPICAL ATMOSPHERE.

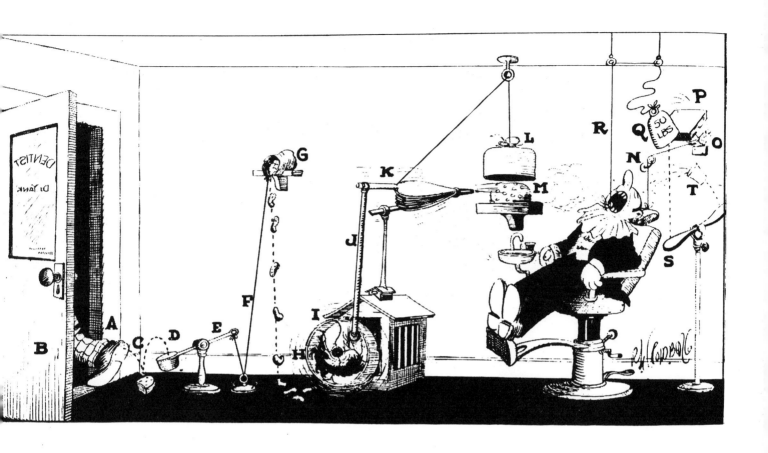

PROFESSOR BUTTS MISTAKES A LOT OF BROKEN
GLASS FOR BATH SALTS AND WHEN THEY PULL
HIM OUT OF THE TUB HE MUMBLES AN IDEA
FOR DODGING BILL COLLECTORS.

AS TAILOR (A) FITS CUSTOMER (B) AND CALLS OU
MEASUREMENTS, COLLEGE BOY (C) MISTAKES
THEM FOR FOOTBALL SIGNALS AND MAKES A
FLYING TACKLE AT CLOTHING DUMMY (D).
DUMMY BUMPS HEAD AGAINST PADDLE (E)
CAUSING IT TO PULL HOOK (F) AND THROW
BOTTLE (G) ON END OF FOLDING HATRACK (H)
WHICH SPREADS AND PUSHES HEAD OF CABBAGE
(I) INTO NET (J). WEIGHT OF CABBAGE PULLS CORD
(K) CAUSING SHEARS (L) TO CUT STRING (M). BAG OF
SAND (N) DROPS ON SCALE (O) AND PUSHES BROOM
(P) AGAINST PAIL OF WHITEWASH (Q) WHICH
UPSETS ALL OVER YOU CAUSING YOU TO LOOK
LIKE A MARBLE STATUE AND MAKING IT
IMPOSSIBLE FOR YOU TO BE RECOGNIZED
BY BILL COLLECTORS.

DON'T WORRY ABOUT POSING AS ANY
PARTICULAR HISTORICAL STATUE BECAUSE
BILL COLLECTORS DON'T KNOW MUCH ABOUT ART

PROFESSOR BUTTS TAKES A DRINK OF STRANGE GIN AND EVOLVES AN INVENTION FOR OPENING THE GARAGE DOOR WITHOUT GETTING OUT OF THE CAR.

DRIVE AUTO BUMPER(A)AGAINST MALLET(B) PUSHING IT DOWN AND EXPLODING CAP(C) FRIGHTENING RABBIT(D)WHO RUNS TOWARD HIS BURROW(E)PULLING STRING (F)WHICH DISCHARGES PISTOL(G). THE BULLET PENETRATES CAN(H)FROM WHICH THE WATER DRIPS INTO AQUARIUM(I). AS THE TIDE RISES IN THE AQUARIUM IT ELEVATES THE FLOATING CORK UPRIGHT(J)WHICH PUSHES UP END OF SEE-SAW(K)CAUSING FLEA(L) TO LOSE IT'S BALANCE AND FALL ON GEDUNK HOUND'S TAIL(M)WHO WAKES UP AND CHASES HIS TAIL ROUND AND ROUND CAUSING PLATFORM(N)TO SPIN AND TURN ON FAUCET(O). WATER RUNS THROUGH HOSE(P)STARTING REVOLVING LAWN SPRINKLER(Q)ON WHICH ROPE (R)WINDS ITSELF OPENING GARAGE DOOR.

OF COURSE, IF YOU WISH, YOU CAN DRIVE RIGHT THROUGH THE DOOR AND THEN THERE WON'T BE ANY OBSTRUCTION LEFT TO BOTHER YOU IN THE FUTURE.

PROFESSOR BUTTS TRIPS OVER A RUG AND, WHILE LOOKING AT THE STARS, DISCOVERS AN IDEA FOR SLICING BREAD FOR THE PICNIC SANDWICH.

RISING SUN(A)RIPENS PEACHES(B)WHICH FALL ON BEEHIVE(C)SCARING OUT BEES WHICH STING SLEEPING INDIVIDUAL(E). SUDDEN PAIN CAUSES HIM TO DOUBLE UP AND KICK LEGS. SPEAR(F)PUNCTURES INNER TUBE(G). PRESSURE OF ESCAPING AIR PUSHES CANNON BALL(H)OFF SHELF(I) KNOCKING OVER SCARECROW(J), WHICH CLUTCHES FARMER(K)FROM THE REAR. FARMER, BELIEVING HE IS BEING ATTACKED BY A BANDIT, STARTS DRIVING HOME LIKE MAD CAUSING DISCS(L)ON DISC-HARROW TO SLICE BREAD(M)IN EVEN PIECES.

THIS INVENTION ISN'T REALLY VERY IMPORTANT BECAUSE SOMEBODY USUALLY GETS BITTEN BY A SNAKE EARLY IN THE DAY AND THE PICNIC BUSTS UP BEFORE YOU GET A CHANCE TO EAT ANY LUNCH.

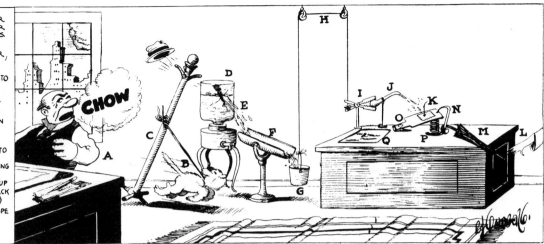

THE MASSIVE INTELLECT OF PROFESSOR BUTTS EVOLVES A SIMPLE APPLIANCE FOR PUTTING POSTAGE STAMPS ON ENVELOPES.

BOSS (A) SNEEZES, SNOZZLEHOUND (B), FRIGHTENED OUT OF A SOUND SLUMBER, RUNS OUT OF THE OFFICE, UPSETTING HATRACK (C) AND BREAKING ICE WATER CONTAINER (D). WATER (E) IS SPILLED INTO TROUGH (F) AND IS THEN CONVEYED TO BUCKET (G).

THE WEIGHT OF THE WATER IN BUCKET CAUSES STRING (H) TO COMPRESS NUT-CRACKER (I) WHICH SQUEEZES BULB ON MEDICINE-DROPPER (J) AND MOISTENS POSTAGE STAMP (K).

STENOGRAPHER (L), ABOUT TO GO OUT TO LUNCH, HEARS THE SPLASHING OF WATER ON SEVERAL OCCASIONS DURING THE OPERATION OF THE APPARATUS. SHE THINKS IT IS RAINING AND PICKS UP HER UMBRELLA (M), WHICH PULLS BACK SMALL HOOK (N), CAUSING SPRING (P) TO THROW PADDLE (O) OVER ON ENVELOPE (Q) AND PRESS MOISTENED STAMP IN PLACE.

THE PROFESSOR TAKES A PILL AND DOPES OUT A DEVICE FOR CLOSING THE WINDOW IF IT STARTS TO RAIN WHILE YOU'RE AWAY.

PET BULL FROG(A), HOMESICK FOR WATER, HEARS RAIN STORM AND JUMPS FOR JOY, PULLING STRING(B) WHICH OPENS CATCH(C) AND RELEASES HOT WATER BAG(D) ALLOWING IT TO SLIDE UNDER CHAIR(E). HEAT RAISES YEAST(F) LIFTING DISK(G) WHICH CAUSES HOOK(H) TO RELEASE SPRING(I). TOY AUTOMOBILE-BUMPER(J) SOCKS MONKEY(K) IN THE NECK PUTTING HIM DOWN FOR THE COUNT ON TABLE(L). HE STAGGERS TO HIS FEET AND SLIPS ON BANANA PEEL(M). HE INSTINCTIVELY REACHES FOR FLYING RINGS(N) TO AVOID FURTHER DISASTER AND HIS WEIGHT PULLS ROPE(O) CLOSING WINDOW(P), STOPPING THE RAIN FROM LEAKING THROUGH ON THE FAMILY DOWNSTAIRS AND THINNING THEIR SOUP.

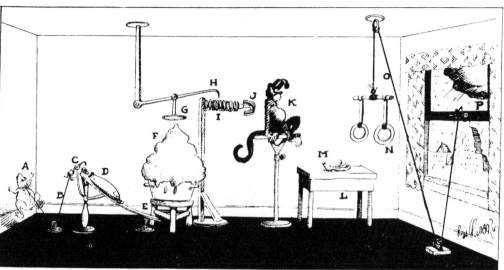

SIMPLE WAY TO CARVE A TURKEY. THIS INVENTION FELL OFF THE PROFESSOR'S HEAD WITH THE REST OF THE DANDRUFF.

PUT BOWL OF CHICKEN SALAD(A) ON WINDOW SILL(B) TO COOL. ROOSTER(C) RECOGNIZES HIS WIFE IN SALAD AND IS OVERCOME WITH GRIEF. HIS TEARS(D) SATURATE SPONGE(E), PULLING STRING(F) WHICH RELEASES TRAP DOOR(G) AND ALLOWS SAND TO RUN DOWN TROUGH(H) INTO PAIL(I). WEIGHT RAISES END OF SEE-SAW(J) WHICH MAKES CORD(K) LIFT COVER OF ICE CREAM FREEZER(L). PENGUIN(M) FEELING CHILL, THINKS HE IS AT THE NORTH POLE AND FLAPS WINGS FOR JOY, THEREBY FANNING PROPELLER(N) WHICH REVOLVES AND TURNS COGS(O) WHICH IN TURN CAUSES TURKEY(P) TO SLIDE BACK AND FORTH OVER CABBAGE-CUTTER UNTIL IT IS SLICED TO A FRAZZLE —

DON'T GET DISCOURAGED IF THE TURKEY GETS PRETTY WELL MESSED UP. IT'S A CINCH IT WOULD HAVE EVENTUALLY BECOME TURKEY HASH ANYWAY.

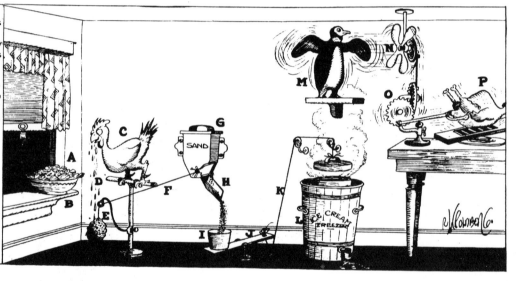

28

PROFESSOR BUTTS GETS CAUGHT IN A REVOLVING DOOR AND BECOMES DIZZY ENOUGH TO DOPE OUT AN IDEA TO KEEP YOU FROM FORGETTING TO MAIL YOUR WIFE'S LETTER.

AS YOU WALK PAST COBBLER SHOP, HOOK STRIKES SUSPENDED BOOT(B) CAUSING IT TO KICK FOOTBALL(C) THROUGH GOAL POSTS(D). FOOTBALL DROPS INTO BASKET(E) AND STRING(F) TILTS SPRINKLING CAN(G) CAUSING WATER TO SOAK COAT TAILS(H). AS COAT SHRINKS CORD(I) OPENS DOOR(J) OF CAGE ALLOWING BIRD(K) TO WALK OUT ON PERCH(L) AND GRAB WORM(M) WHICH IS ATTACHED TO STRING(N). THIS PULLS DOWN WINDOW SHADE(O) ON WHICH IS WRITTEN, "YOU SAP, MAIL THAT LETTER." A SIMPLE WAY TO AVOID ALL THIS TROUBLE IS TO MARRY A WIFE WHO CAN'T WRITE.

THE PROFESSOR TURNS ON HIS THINK-FAUCET AND DOPES OUT A MACHINE FOR WASHING DISHES WHILE YOU ARE AT THE MOVIES.

WHEN SPOILED TOMCAT (A) DISCOVERS HE IS ALONE HE LETS OUT A YELL WHICH SCARES MOUSE (B) INTO JUMPING INTO BASKET (C), CAUSING LEVER END (D) TO RISE AND PULL STRING (E) WHICH SNAPS AUTOMATIC CIGAR LIGHTER (F). FLAME (G) STARTS FIRE SPRINKLER (H). WATER RUNS ON DISHES (I) AND DRIPS INTO SINK (J). TURTLE (K), THINKING HE HEARS BABBLING BROOK BABBLING, AND HAVING NO SENSE OF DIRECTION, STARTS WRONG WAY AND PULLS STRING (L), WHICH TURNS ON SWITCH (M) THAT STARTS ELECTRIC GLOW HEATER (N). HEAT RAY (O) DRIES THE DISHES.

IF THE CAT AND THE TURTLE GET ON TO YOUR SCHEME AND REFUSE TO COOPERATE, SIMPLY PUT THE DISHES ON THE FRONT PORCH AND PRAY FOR RAIN.

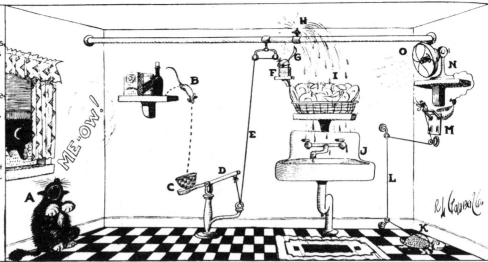

A SAFE FALLS ON THE HEAD OF PROFESSOR BUTTS AND KNOCKS OUT AN IDEA FOR HIS LATEST SIMPLE FLY SWATTER.

CARBOLIC ACID (A) DRIPS ON STRING (B) CAUSING IT TO BREAK AND RELEASE ELASTIC OF BEAN SHOOTER (C) WHICH PROJECTS BALL (D) INTO BUNCH OF GARLIC (E) CAUSING IT TO FALL INTO SYRUP CAN (F) AND SPLASH SYRUP VIOLENTLY AGAINST SIDE WALL. FLY (G) BUZZES WITH GLEE AND GOES FOR SYRUP, HIS FAVORITE DISH. BUTLER-DOG (H) MISTAKES HUM OF FLY'S WINGS FOR DOOR BUZZER AND RUNS TO MEET VISITOR, PULLING ROPE (I) WHICH TURNS STOP-GO SIGNAL (J) AND CAUSES BASEBALL BAT (K) TO SOCK FLY WHO FALLS TO FLOOR UNCONSCIOUS.

AS FLY DROPS TO FLOOR PET TROUT (L) JUMPS FOR HIM, MISSES, AND LANDS IN NET (M). WEIGHT OF FISH FORCES SHOE (N) DOWN ON FALLEN FLY AND PUTS HIM OUT OF THE RUNNING FOR ALL TIME.

IF THE FISH CATCHES THE FLY, THE SHOE CAN BE USED FOR CRACKING NUTS.

The Professor takes a swig of Goofy Oil and invents the self-sharpening razor blade —

Wind blows open door (A), pulling string (B) which causes hammer (C) to explode cap (D). Peaceful cockroach (E) loses balance from fright and falls into pail of water (F). Water splashes on washboard (G), soap (H) slides over surface, pulling string (I), yanking out prop from under shelf (J) and upsetting bowl (K). Goldfish (L) fall into bath tub (M) and hungry seagull (N) swoops down on them, thereby pulling string (O) which turns on switch (P), starting motor (Q) and causing razor blade (R) to move up and down along strop (S).

It is advisable to live near a barber shop in case there is no wind to blow the door open in the first place.

Automatic suicide device for unlucky stock speculators — when phone (A) rings, it is probably a message from your broker saying you are wiped out — phone bell wakes up office manager (B) who stretches, hitting lever (C) and starting toy glider (D) which nosedives and hits head of dwarf (E) — he jumps up and down from pain, working handle of jack (F), lifting pig (G) to level of potato (H) on end of bookkeeper's collar button (I) — pig eats potato and motion of collar button annoys bookkeeper who moves head forward with sudden jerk causing string (J) to shoot off gun (K) and end your troubles — If telephone call is not from broker, you'll never find out the mistake because you'll be dead anyway.

PROFESSOR BUTTS TRIPS OVER A HAZARD ON A MINIATURE GOLF COURSE AND LANDS ON AN IDEA FOR AN AUTOMATIC DEVICE FOR EMPTYING ASH TRAYS.

BRIGHT FULL MOON (A) CAUSES LOVE BIRDS (B) TO BECOME ROMANTIC AND AS THEY GET TOGETHER THEIR WEIGHT CAUSES PERCH (C) TO TIP AND PULL STRING (D) WHICH UPSETS CAN (E) AND SPRINKLES WOOLEN SHIRT (F) CAUSING IT TO SHRINK AND DRAW ASIDE CURTAIN EXPOSING PORTRAIT OF WIGWAG PUP'S MASTER (G). AS PUP (H) SEES MASTER'S PICTURE HE WIGWAGS TAIL FOR JOY AND UPSETS ASH TRAY (I), SPILLING ASHES AND SMOULDERING BUTTS INTO ASBESTOS BAG (J) ATTACHED TO SKY ROCKET (K). BUTT (L), PASSING FUSE (M), IGNITES IT AND CAUSES ROCKET TO SHOOT OUT OF WINDOW DISPOSING OF ASHES.

YOU SHOULD ALWAYS HAVE TWENTY OR THIRTY HIGH-POWERED AEROPLANES READY TO GO OUT AND SEARCH FOR THE ASBESTOS BAG.

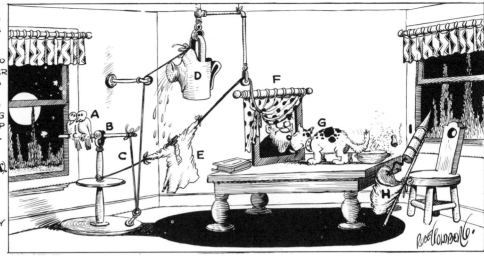

FOOLISH QUESTIONS NO. 47,389,100

IS THAT A CAT?

MEOW

NO, IT'S A MULE GIVING AN IMITATION OF A MOCKING BIRD

DEVICE FOR KEEPING RING RIGHT IN FRONT OF GROOM'S NOSE.

SPECIAL HIGH HAT TO CATCH RICE — BRIDE MAKES RICE PUDDING, GIVING GROOM INDIGESTION AND STARTING FIRST FIGHT.

MARCH 15, 1967 / FIFTY CENTS

FORBES

AFTER COLOR TV?
The future of home entertainment

RUBE GOLDBERG

32

AUTOMATIC HAMMER TO PUT FISH OUT OF MISERY AS HE GRABS HOOK.

ELECTRIC MOSQUITO-SLAPPER.

MAGNIFYING GLASS FRONT FOR MOUNTED FISH.

AUTOMATIC FOOT FOR KICKING BALL OUT OF SAND-TRAP — IT WORKS WITH MOTION OF ARM WHILE TRYING TO LIGHT PIPE.

SODA-CRACKER SCORE CARD — IF YOU'RE AFRAID SOMEBODY WILL SEE YOUR SCORE, YOU CAN EAT IT!

GREEN TOUPE WHICH FALLS OFF YOUR HEAD INTO HOLE MADE BY DIVOT, KEEPING COURSE IN PERFECT SHAPE!

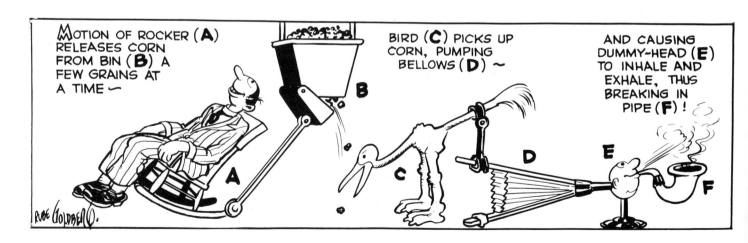

MOTION OF ROCKER (A) RELEASES CORN FROM BIN (B) A FEW GRAINS AT A TIME —

BIRD (C) PICKS UP CORN, PUMPING BELLOWS (D) —

AND CAUSING DUMMY-HEAD (E) TO INHALE AND EXHALE, THUS BREAKING IN PIPE (F)!

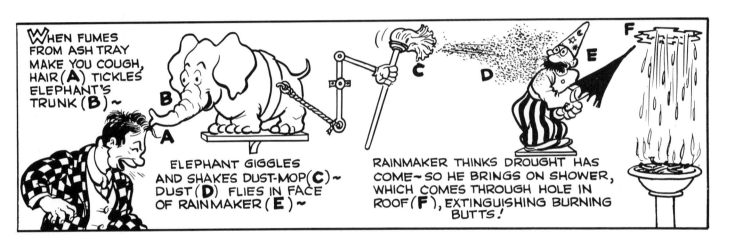

35

HOW TO REMOVE HAT WHEN ARMS ARE PINNED TO YOUR SIDES

WIGGLE EARS TO RELEASE HOOKS — SPRING RAISES HAT.

SMALL CAR WITH SKI STICKS FOR CATCHING ELEVATOR BEFORE IT GOES PAST YOUR FLOOR.

LUNCH SERVICE FOR PASSENGERS MAROONED IN REAR OF CROWDED ELEVATOR FOR DAYS.

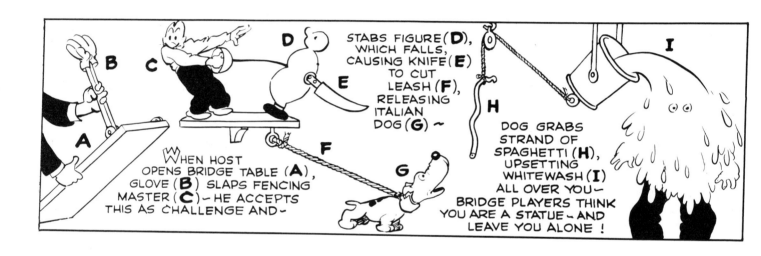

WHEN HOST OPENS BRIDGE TABLE (A), GLOVE (B) SLAPS FENCING MASTER (C) — HE ACCEPTS THIS AS CHALLENGE AND —

STABS FIGURE (D), WHICH FALLS, CAUSING KNIFE (E) TO CUT LEASH (F), RELEASING ITALIAN DOG (G) ~

DOG GRABS STRAND OF SPAGHETTI (H), UPSETTING WHITEWASH (I) ALL OVER YOU — BRIDGE PLAYERS THINK YOU ARE A STATUE — AND LEAVE YOU ALONE !

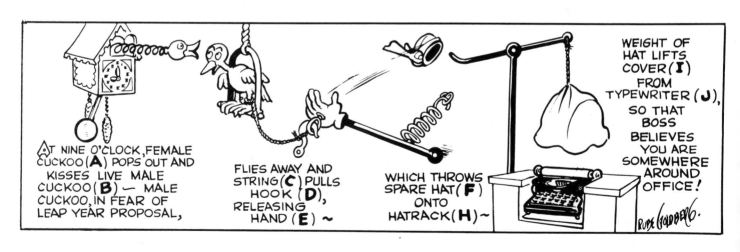

AT NINE O'CLOCK, FEMALE CUCKOO (A) POPS OUT AND KISSES LIVE MALE CUCKOO (B) — MALE CUCKOO, IN FEAR OF LEAP YEAR PROPOSAL,

FLIES AWAY AND STRING (C) PULLS HOOK (D), RELEASING HAND (E) ~

WHICH THROWS SPARE HAT (F) ONTO HATRACK (H) ~

WEIGHT OF HAT LIFTS COVER (I) FROM TYPEWRITER (J), SO THAT BOSS BELIEVES YOU ARE SOMEWHERE AROUND OFFICE !

RUBE GOLDBERG.

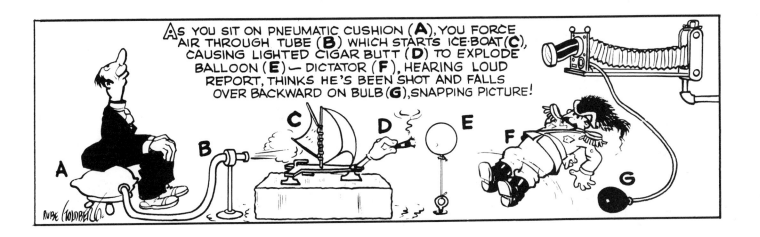

AS YOU SIT ON PNEUMATIC CUSHION (**A**), YOU FORCE AIR THROUGH TUBE (**B**) WHICH STARTS ICE-BOAT (**C**), CAUSING LIGHTED CIGAR BUTT (**D**) TO EXPLODE BALLOON (**E**) — DICTATOR (**F**), HEARING LOUD REPORT, THINKS HE'S BEEN SHOT AND FALLS OVER BACKWARD ON BULB (**G**), SNAPPING PICTURE!

A
MOTH'S MOTHER WARNS IT TO KEEP AWAY FROM FLAME ~

B
YOUNG MOTH, HEEDING ADVICE OF FOND PARENT, TAKES ROAD UP HILL TO LEFT, WORKING UP APPETITE ~

THIS WAY TO OVERCOAT

C
MOTH STEPS ON BUTTON, TURNING ON WINDSHIELD-WIPER ~

D
WHEN DUST IS REMOVED FROM WINDSHIELD, MOTH SEES OVERCOAT AND MAKES DASH FOR IT, KNOCKING OUT BRAINS AGAINST GLASS !

WOMAN, SEEING MOUSE, JUMPS ON PNEUMATIC CUSHION (**A**) — ESCAPING AIR MAKES NOISE LIKE HOG-CALL (**B**)

OINK

HOG (**C**) STIRS HIMSELF AND SPLASHES MUD (**D**) IN EYE OF MIDGET MARATHON RUNNER (**E**) ~

WHO LOSES WAY AND RUNS INTO DISC (**F**), GIVING HAND (**G**) A SUDDEN PUSH ~

FOUNTAIN PEN (**H**) SHAKES INK AGAINST WALL (**I**) — MOUSE THINKS INKSPOT IS HOLE IN WALL AND TRIES TO RUN THROUGH IT, DASHING OUT BRAINS !

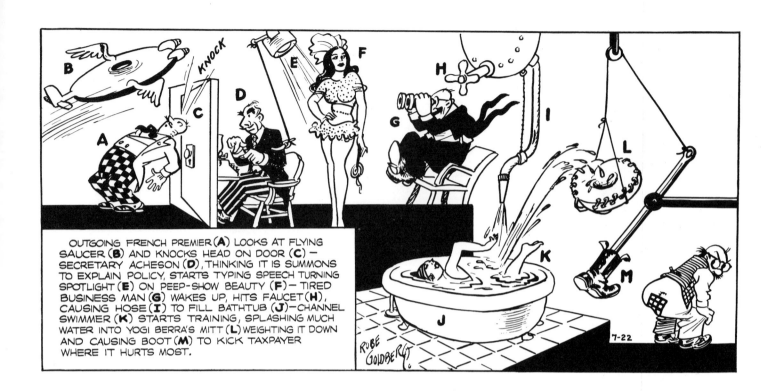

OUTGOING FRENCH PREMIER (**A**) LOOKS AT FLYING SAUCER (**B**) AND KNOCKS HEAD ON DOOR (**C**) — SECRETARY ACHESON (**D**), THINKING IT IS SUMMONS TO EXPLAIN POLICY, STARTS TYPING SPEECH TURNING SPOTLIGHT (**E**) ON PEEP-SHOW BEAUTY (**F**) — TIRED BUSINESS MAN (**G**) WAKES UP, HITS FAUCET (**H**), CAUSING HOSE (**I**) TO FILL BATHTUB (**J**) — CHANNEL SWIMMER (**K**) STARTS TRAINING, SPLASHING MUCH WATER INTO YOGI BERRA'S MITT (**L**) WEIGHTING IT DOWN AND CAUSING BOOT (**M**) TO KICK TAXPAYER WHERE IT HURTS MOST.

7-22

OUR LATEST SIMPLE ALARM CLOCK

ELEANOR (**A**) RECITES "PETER AND THE WOLF" — CHILD (**B**) FIDGETS, AND MOTHER (**C**) SPANKS HIM, TURNING FAUCET (**D**) FOR GOOF (**E**) TO GO OVER NIAGARA FALLS (**F**) IN BARREL, CAUSING WATER WHEEL (**G**) TO TURN KEY, LOCKING UP HARRY BRIDGES (**H**), WHO RATTLES BARS, SHAKING BASKET (**I**) AND LETTING OUT MOTHS (**J**) — MOTHS START TO EAT BATHING SUIT OF MISS LAS VEGAS (**K**), WHO CAUSES WHIP (**L**) TO START NAG (**M**) IN FOURTH RACE AT SARATOGA — NAG FALLS INTO U.N. RED TAPE (**N**), CAUSING FEATHER (**O**) TO TICKLE ELECTRIC EEL (**P**), WHOSE SPARKS EXPLODE BOMB (**Q**), KILLING SABOTEUR (**R**) AND BLOWING YOU OUT OF BED (**S**) IN TIME TO GO TO WORK SO YOU CAN PAY MORE TAXES.

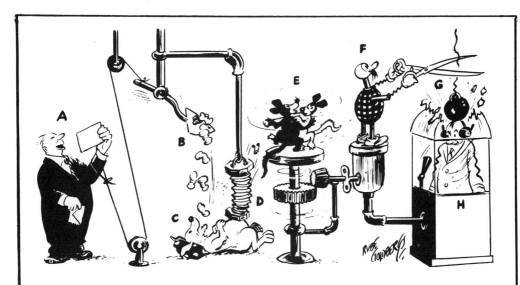

QUIZMASTER (**A**) RAISES HAND TO READ QUESTION, DROPPING SHOVELFUL OF DOG BISCUITS (**B**) INTO MOUTH OF RECLINING DOG (**C**) — DOG GOES TO SLEEP FROM OVEREATING AND HEAVY BREATHING PLAYS DANCE MUSIC ON ACCORDIAN (**D**) — WALTZING MICE (**E**) REVOLVE VIOLENTLY, CAUSING MECHANICAL BARBER (**F**) TO CUT STRING, DROPPING IRON BALL (**G**) ON CONTESTANT (**H**), RENDERING HIM UNABLE TO ANSWER QUESTION, THUS KEEPING PROGRAM FREE FROM CORRUPTION.

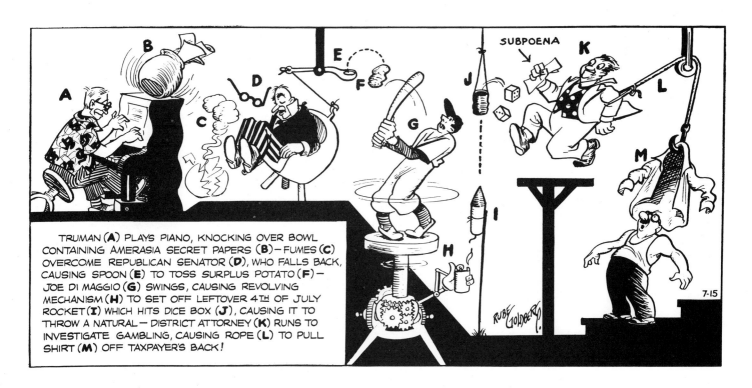

TRUMAN (**A**) PLAYS PIANO, KNOCKING OVER BOWL CONTAINING AMERASIA SECRET PAPERS (**B**) — FUMES (**C**) OVERCOME REPUBLICAN SENATOR (**D**), WHO FALLS BACK, CAUSING SPOON (**E**) TO TOSS SURPLUS POTATO (**F**) — JOE DI MAGGIO (**G**) SWINGS, CAUSING REVOLVING MECHANISM (**H**) TO SET OFF LEFTOVER 4TH OF JULY ROCKET (**I**) WHICH HITS DICE BOX (**J**), CAUSING IT TO THROW A NATURAL — DISTRICT ATTORNEY (**K**) RUNS TO INVESTIGATE GAMBLING, CAUSING ROPE (**L**) TO PULL SHIRT (**M**) OFF TAXPAYER'S BACK!

7-15

HOW TO KEEP DOWN THE DIVORCE RATE

COPY OF RUSSIAN "PRAVDA" (**A**) BLOWS IN WINDOW AND
LANDS IN LIE-DETECTOR (**B**), WHICH EXPLODES, PUNCTURING BAG
OF ERROL FLYNN'S ALIMONY (**C**) — COINS (**D**) DROP IN BELGIAN CROWN
(**E**), CAUSING BOOT (**F**) TO KICK MOBSTER MICKEY COHEN (**G**) INTO
ANOTHER TOWN. HUNTER (**H**), MISTAKING MICKEY FOR A DUCK,
SHOOTS AND MISSES, BUT HITS STARTER ON CRANE (**I**), CAUSING
ROPE (**J**) TO LOWER BOTTLE OF MILK (**K**) TO NEW BRITISH
ROYAL BABY (**L**) — BABY ROCKS WITH GLEE, UNROLLING RED
TOWEL (**M**) — MAD BULL (**N**), ENTERTAINING NEW AMBASSADOR
TO MEXICO BILL O'DWYER, ATTACKS TOWEL, CAUSING HOOK (**O**)
TO PULL HOUSEWIFE (**P**) AWAY FROM CANASTA TABLE, THUS
KEEPING HER HUSBAND FROM SUING FOR DESERTION.

HENRY WALLACE (**A**) DOES A POLITICAL SOMERSAULT,
KNOCKING LEFTIE FRIEND (**B**) OFF BALANCE — FRIEND
REACHES FOR STRING (**C**), UNVEILING BAG OF SUGAR (**D**) —
HOARDING HOUSEWIFE (**E**) RUNS ON TREADMILL (**F**) FOR
SUGAR, CAUSING HAND (**G**) TO STRUM ARTHUR
GODFREY'S UKULELE (**H**) — VEEP BARKLEY (**I**) DOES A
CHARLESTON, KICKING TRIGGER OF NEW SUPER-
BAZOOKA (**J**), WHICH SHOOTS ROPE (**K**), ALLOWING
HEAVY BUCKET OF TYDINGS-MCCARTHY MUD (**L**) TO
DROP ON VISE HANDLE (**M**), GIVING TAXPAYER (**N**)
THE USUAL SQUEEZE!

To Sum Up:

Rube Goldberg's New-Career machine, drawn especially for NEWSWEEK: "Father Time (A) lifts lid of magic box (B). releasing spring which causes candle (C) to burn string (D) and drop iron boot (E) on Democratic donkey (F). Donkey kicks Republican elephant (G) which snorts in anger and blows cannonball (H) into Uncle Sam's hat (I), thereby lifting me (J) away from my drawing board into the 'higher art' of sculpture."

I'm the guy with blonde hair parted in the middle, aged fifteen. The others are my sister Lillian, my older brother Garry, the real humorist in the family then, and my brother Walter, eight years my junior. Garry put away his ventriloquist's dummy, went straight, and did well in the wholesale paint business in California.

2

In 1899 or thereabouts, the Max Goldbergs of San Francisco were holding daily powwows on a problem which to them seemed second to none in world importance: What were they going to do about Reuben? Was the second son of the family, then sixteen years old, going to get away with that silly idea he had about becoming an artist? Here the Goldberg family had been good, useful citizens for generations, and now one of them was set on blotching the escutcheon. It was all very dreadful and nobody was more heavy-hearted than Pa Goldberg.

"For the honor of the family don't do this awful thing, Rube," he pleaded. "Think of how I'm going to feel when I say to somebody 'This is my son,' and then a long-haired freak steps forward. Rube, let me tell you something," he became very serious, "maybe the Goldbergs haven't the wealth or style of the Astors, but they're just as honorable. We've always come clean and we can look anybody in the eye. Be reasonable."

When a baseball pitcher goes left-handed it's taken as a sign that he's not altogether there, and so they nickname him Rube. This Rube was a southpaw, so he qualified for membership in the clan. Unmoved by the plea of Pa Goldberg, he said:

"I wanna be an artist. When people come to the house I'll hide in the cellar. And I promise that any time I have a quarter I'll get a haircut."

But Max Goldberg, fire-insurance broker, police commissioner, Golden Gate politician, and owner of an Arizona cattle ranch, was obdurate. If the impending ignominy could be staved off he was determined to stave it.

Fate works in mysterious ways. It chanced that the Guggenheims hired John Hays Hammond as the engineer in charge of their mining interests, at a salary reported at $1,000,000 a year. That stupendous contract was the business sensation of the day. It focused attention on the potential earning power of an engineer and got it into the minds of thousands of fathers that here was a profession their sons might well adopt. The schools teaching mining engineering became magnets.

Pa Goldberg had a happy thought. An engineer had to be a draftsman and Rube was bent on drawing. Why couldn't Rube find an outlet for this ambition in a practical way? Given the right technical training, plus his natural leanings, he might some day be able to draw as well as Mr. Hammond was drawing in the way of salary.

Pa Goldberg said: "You win, Rube. I guess the best thing to do is to let a boy follow his own inclinations when it comes to choosing a career."

"That's great, pa. Do you think I should start as the cartoonist for *The Chronicle?*"

"No! I want you to do this thing on a big scale. If you promise to work hard I'll let you study art under some real masters. What would you say if I told you you could become a student at the mining engineering school at the University of California?"

"Mining engineering! What's that got to do with studying art?"

Max Goldberg acted aghast at such stupidity. "Why, my boy, don't you know that all the great artists, such as Da Vinci and Homer Davenport and Fred Opper and Rembrandt and Tad Dorgan, spent years studying mining engineering before they ever lifted a brush? You can never hope to be a real artist until you've learned mining engineering. Look at Mr. Hammond! He's getting a million dollars a year already. Think of the future in store for him when he feels enough confidence in himself to branch out as an artist."

It was not so much the reference to Da Vinci and Rembrandt that struck home as it was his explanation of why Opper and Tad had become famous. For one of my birthdays, somebody had made me a present of one of the Bill Nye collections of humor, illustrated by Opper. It was a family legend that the cute little toddler spent the day tracing the drawings on the tissue paper of his mother's dress patterns, cleverly plucked from their hiding place in the dining-room china closet.

Stage people love to dwell affectionately on the "smell" of grease paint. There is a pungent aroma to every art. One of my earliest thrills was the "smell" of cartoons. My older brother at the age of twelve earned a few extra pennies on Saturdays delivering magazines to barber shops. On days when he was indisposed he turned his route over to me. I shall never forget the excitement I experienced when I took hold of a bundle of those magazines, among which were *Puck, Judge, Life,* and *Leslie's,* and inhaled the fragrant aroma of printer's ink, galloping over the shiny pages in the intriguing shapes of humorous figures by T. S. Sullivant, Albert Levering, Joseph Keppler, Bernhard Gillam, F. W. Howarth, and others.

My father the cattle-rancher and police commissioner, with my brother and me. I'm the dandy at right.

44

In succeeding years I supplemented my admiration for the funny sketches of Opper with a species of fanatical worship for the pen-and-ink genius of Zim (Eugene Zimmerman), Tad (T. A. Dorgan), Charles Dana Gibson and Walter Appleton Clark.

I was just eleven years old when a playmate in San Francisco plotted with me to take drawing lessons from a sign painter who agreed to inculcate the rudiments of art at fifty cents a lesson. Charles Beall painted signs, but at heart he was an artist. He was painstaking and conscientious, he was not a man who considered his work lightly. He believed in doing good work, even on a sign.

Mr. Beall permitted no slipshod work and no loafing. He taught us that whatever we did was worth doing well. The chum who seduced me into taking drawing lessons was George Wagner, who became one of the leading architects of San Francisco. We were very much in earnest. But my parents were not very enthusiastic, either about having an artist in the family, or about permitting an eleven-year-old boy

SENSATIONAL INVENTING. — You Must Be a " Wizard " to Attract Attention.

This prophetic cartoon in *Puck*, 1889, was by Frederick Burr Opper, who had set me tracing his illustrations for Bill Nye stories. Nye's burlesque *History of the United States* was the biggest bestseller of that humorist's fourteen books. A Nye biographer credited Opper drawings with making up for "the shortcomings of the text." Some other books of Nye's were illustrated by another man whose works I admired when an embryonic cartoonist, "Zim" (Eugene Zimmerman).

45

to be out late at night. But they saw I was determined to draw, so they consented to let me try — merely cautioning me to make the trial a thorough one.

I was only twelve years old when my first picture was exhibited — and for a few weeks I felt as if I would have called Michelangelo "Mike" if he had been around. It was a pen and ink drawing, a picture of an old violinist, and was shown at the old John Swett grammar school. Then it was hung in the Board of Education rooms to show what the pupils could do. Eventually it was hung in my father's home.

For three years George and I went to Mr. Beall's home every Friday evening, without missing a lesson. We drew in pen and ink, charcoal, and pencil; and we painted in water-colors and in oil. Those Friday nights were heaven for me. The rest of the week consisted largely in waiting for Friday night.

I thought we were learning Art (I always thought of it with a capital), and did not realize that we merely were laying a solid foundation upon which to build. It was very serious work. Fact is, I was a very serious sort of kid.

Of my parents' four surviving children (three were lost in infancy), my oldest brother, Garrett, was the humorist of the family. Garry did card tricks; he did monologues (with jokes from books he bought by mail) and he was an accomplished ventriloquist. In family entertainments, with my mother, sister Lillian, and brother Walter as audience, Garry played violin, I was at piano, and my father strummed banjo. My father had quite a repertoire of old Western songs. I remember one he sang, entitled *Liza Jane,* about a California mining-camp Calamity Jane. It began:

> *Her mouth was like a cellar door,*
> *Her face was like a ham.*

It was ridicule I feared above all things. The memory of the suffering and humiliation I felt at that time, if anyone ridiculed me or my work, has made me much more kindly, I hope, in poking fun at others. While I was to deal largely in ridicule in my cartoons I never believed in the brand which sears. I never have ridiculed the *individual.*

At that time, when the others were doing funny stunts I used to think of lots funnier ones that I might have done — a minute or two too late to do them even if I'd had the courage. That period, while painful, was valuable. I commenced to study people; sometimes with the intention of imitating them — which I lacked the nerve to carry out. Shy, untalkative persons are usually the best observers. If you do not believe it, talk to some shy fourteen-year-old girl and learn what she has seen and heard while the others were chattering and giggling.

If ever there is a time when a human being

My artistic triumph when I was twelve: the pen and ink drawing I copied from a lithograph entitled "The Old Violinist." It was exhibited to show what students in San Francisco public schools could do.

46

needs kind treatment and understanding advice, it is at that age, when a word of criticism or ridicule may curdle his disposition or wreck his career. Even today I cannot understand how boys of that age have the nerve to show their work. Sometimes one comes to my studio, shows his pictures, explains them unblushingly, and tells his plans. At that age, wild with desire as I was, I never would have dared enter a newspaper office, or shown my work to anyone except some confidential chum. I wanted to hide it. And even today, after years as an artist, I feel uneasy when anyone looks at an unfinished work.

Myself the soldier, University of California cadet corps. The Spanish-American War had been brought to a conclusion before I was sixteen years old.

My cartoon in 1903 Yearbook won a prize. The football gladiators, wearing the customary noseguards of that era, represent University of California and a challenging upstart, Stanford University.

1903
"A Dead Heat"

So assiduously did I study that by the time I was ready to enter Lowell High School I had learned to draw fairly well. The high school paper published my drawings, and though the editors meant no harm by it, they were largely responsible for what's happened to me since then. For once I had appeared on the printed page all hope was gone for being like other people. Every time the school paper came from the press and I saw my drawings reproduced I felt sorry that everybody couldn't be as talented as I was.

Yet my father's talk convinced me that the only way anybody could ever get to be a great artist was to follow in the footsteps of John Hays Hammond. So I became a student of mining engineering at the University of California and assumed a tolerant attitude toward physics, chemistry and trigonometry.

Really the best break I had as a student in the College of Mining came when Carleton Parker, one of the undergraduates, started a campus paper called *The Pelican*, which was one of the first college comic publications. I made a lot of pen-and-ink sketches for *The Pelican*, and Parker was kind enough to publish them. After several of them had appeared and Parker had said they weren't as terrible as you might think, I came to the conclusion that the effort to make a mining engineer of me wasn't a total loss. This conviction was strengthened when, in my senior year, I won a prize for a poster. The prize carried with it a trip to the Yosemite Valley, but with the consent of the editors I went to Los Angeles instead.

One of the great unfathomed mysteries of the University of California is how I managed to skim through my final examinations and receive a diploma. Graduate I did, 1904, in spite of myself, and I now stepped forth into the world with only one specific thought, which was that of all the hocus-pocus the world had to offer, the outstanding myth was the glory of mining engineering. About the subterfuge of that profession being linked with art I was now thoroughly disillusioned. If the Guggenheims had at that moment raised John Hays Hammond's salary to $2,000,000 a year I would still have been willing to exchange my diploma for one clean sheet of Bristol board.

Anxious to salvage something out of the situation, which had taken three and a half years to prove itself a failure as far as its original purpose went, I took a job as draftsman under Thomas P. Woodward, the San Francisco city engineer and a friend of my father, at one hundred dollars a month. My task was mapping sewer pipes and water mains, and I found it as interesting as it sounds.

It was a struggle between love and duty — or rather between desire and common sense — for three months. I became so blue and discouraged that all doubt ended. Nothing but art work ever would satisfy me. So I went home one night and said:

"Dad, I can't stand it any longer; I'm going to quit."

Fortunately, I possessed the right sort of father: one who understood. Perhaps he, in boyhood, had been compelled to give up some career he had cherished. Had he objected I never should have had the courage to oppose his wishes.

However, my university career was not entirely wasted. I got a job on the San Francisco *Chronicle*, because the city editor, whose son had gone to the "U," had seen *Pelicans* in which my drawings appeared. That little experience proves that college friendships can be the most valuable part of a college career. At least, they last long after everything else gained there is forgotten.

Up to that time my life had been soft. There had been no occasion for me to make a fight for myself; and consequently no one knew whether it was in me *to* fight. Dad wisely decided to find out. My pay as a beginner — an office boy — in the art department of *The Chronicle* was eight dollars a week, and for a while every time I was paid I felt guilty because of taking pay for doing something I loved to do. But no one ever put in a more bitterly discouraging period than my first three months in that art department. The workers were good fellows; but I was a kid, and a rube, and they loved to tease. For three months I drew pictures and not one drawing ever appeared in the paper! They went into the waste basket; which perhaps is where they belonged. But imagine the torture to a sensitive boy to see his work thrown away, day after day!

The incident that turned the tide turned out to be funny. One of the editors had a son who was running in a track meet at Berkeley Prep. The event was not important, except to the editor's son and the editor's son's father, who ordered the sports editor to send an artist over to make a picture of the race. The sports editor did not want to waste a real artist, so he sent me.

The assignment was a great event in my life. I spent the morning fixing my drawing board, sharpening pencils, putting in fresh pens, and arranging the desk so as to go to work as soon as I could get back. The paper was measured and ruled; the ink set right.

After the meet I dashed back with my sketches. . . . The desk had been cleared. Everything had been stuffed into the drawers, which were nailed tight — and all the artists were gone. I could have cried, or fought, or done anything! I knew I was done for; but I determined to get even. So I went out, bought hammer and nails, and nailed up every desk drawer in the art department.

The next morning I expected trouble. Instead, men in the art department welcomed me as a friend and a brother. A kid who had nerve enough to fight back was their idea of the kind of fellow they wanted; and from that day on I "belonged." The next day my first cartoon appeared.

M. H. De Young of *The Chronicle,* who bore the courtesy title of "Colonel," had undergone a change of heart about newspaper comics. Aside from the Sunday colored supplements, the only pen-and-ink drawings most newspapers had much use for in those days were political cartoons. These were usually run on the editorial or front pages. Colonel De Young had told my father after I went to work at *The Chronicle* that he didn't see much of a future for the newspaper comic artist and that he thought it would be better for me to engage in some more substantial work. But now he was more tolerant toward these features; it was likely that the space competing papers now devoted to them had something to do with his revised judgment.

The sporting page began coming into its own as a reader attraction simultaneously with the increasing popularity of the comic. Sports had always been looked upon as a sort of necessary evil in most newspaper shops — a come-on to the low-brows — and the space allotted to them was seldom more than a full page, if that much.

My first real chance came when Tad Dorgan left the San Francisco *Bulletin* to go East. I made such a pest of myself asking for the position that Hy Baggerly, *The Bulletin's* sports editor, gave it to me in self-defense. I learned two lessons at once: first, the difficulty any man has in succeeding a popular worker; and, second, that individuality is the thing that counts.

The paper devoted a great deal of attention to sports pictures. Baggerly sent me off to prizefight training camps to make "action" sketches and he also asked me to write something to go with each batch of these. One of my secret ambitions, which I never had dared confess, was to learn to write — which I never had attempted for publication. Now I commenced to write in the vein of the pictures; a sort of mild, semi-sarcastic ridicule, not of individuals but of situations and action.

The stuff was different and the readers liked it for that reason. I went around among strangers, listening to get their ideas of the stories and pictures. I enjoyed writing, but al-

Here, and in two following pages, examples of my cartoons for the *San Francisco Chronicle,* 1906, when numerous get-rich-quick families were getting daughters European titles the hard money way. The second was an attempt in my usual sports page space to see something on the bright side after the disaster of April 18-21, razed about a third of the city. Many homeless did camp out at the Presidio and Golden Gate Park for a while.

WHAT MOST SPORTING MEN ARE DOING NOW — LIVING THE SIMPLE LIFE CLOSE TO NATURE

THE CANDLE LIGHT IS
HARD ON THE DOPESTERS
(OPTICIANS TAKE NOTICE)

THE CROSS MARKS THE SPOT
WHERE HE HAD HIS LAST BEER.

IN THE BREAD LINE

SOME OF THE BASEBALL FANS
HAVE THE HABIT SO BAD
THEY CAN'T KEEP AWAY
FROM THE GROUNDS

THE OLD BOYS WILL HAVE
THEIR LITTLE SAY

ways found that drawing had the stronger "pull," or appeal, for me.

Then the New York bug bit me. I had read stuff about New York recognizing talent and sending for it. I waited a year for the call to come from New York. *The Bulletin* was paying me thirty dollars a week when I announced I was quitting. *The Bulletin* offered to boost me to fifty dollars a week if I would stay, but even my father's intervention couldn't induce me to change my mind. I was completely sold on the idea that the big city was the one place where a fellow in my line had a chance to make good in a national way. A collection of originals adorning the walls of a San Francisco club had cast a spell over me. They included drawings by Homer Davenport, Tom Powers, Bob Edgren, Jimmy Swinnerton. The "Little Bears" Swinnerton had made daily characters in *The Examiner* he transformed into "Little Tigers" when he went East. I spent fascinated hours in studying all the collection. It was of the utmost significance to me that their creators were located in New York.

I was twenty-three, I had waited long enough. I thought of the Biblical saying: "Many are called, but few are chosen." It seemed to me that none were called, and that was that.

Harry Mayo Bunker, who had put me through a merciless hazing when I was breaking in at *The Chronicle,* had preceded me to New York, and I let him know of my purposeful advent. He met me on arrival and invited me to put up at his studio in the old Lincoln Arcade Building, Broadway at Sixty-sixth Street. I soon discovered that Bunker's quarters were a favorite rendezvous for New York newspaper night owls. Nearly every night a bunch of them were there for a poker session.

Three of the regulars were Tad, who had been brought East by W. R. Hearst as a New York *Journal* cartoonist; his brother, Ike, then a sporting writer on the same paper, and Henry Raleigh, the illustrator for magazines. The games were as quiet as a riveters' picnic. The gamesmanship of the players seemed to be that the one who could shout loudest and pound furniture the hardest stood the best chance of winning. Tad excelled in this respect. I would wake up at four A.M. with the floor shaking, to see a poker sharp holding a full house, and singing *Sweet Adeline.* I thought how tame the San Francisco earthquake, which I survived, had been.

I had asked Bunker how I should go about connecting with a New York paper, and he had told me not to be in a hurry about trying. Though I didn't appreciate it at the time, his object in advising me to take it easy was to stave off as long as possible the punishment he knew I was in for. People of Park Row, where newspaper publishing was centered in those days, maintained all sorts of game laws to guard the older denizens from extinction at the hands of aspiring Nimrods. One of the familiar sights along the Row was a meek-faced youth walking into a newspaper office with his precious sketches and walking out again in dejection.

The Morning Telegraph was my first approach. I told the boy at the gate to say to Irving Lewis, the executive editor, that Mr. Goldberg of San Francisco wished to see him. The boy looked doubtfully at the bundle I was carrying — it looked like a roll of blankets — as he went inside with the message that did get me an interview.

"Now just supposing there was an opening here, which there isn't — but supposing there was — what could you do for *The Morning Telegraph?*" Mr. Lewis asked.

"I thought I might be able to improve the paper."

Lewis gasped. There was a gun lying on his desk and he seemed so outraged by my impertinence I thought for a moment he'd pick it up.

"So you think this paper needs improvement and that you're the boy wonder who can do it! Well, young man, we have the best men in the market and we can get plenty more like them."

With that he marched me off to the newspaper's "morgue" and proudly exhibited back files of *The Telegraph* as convincers. Being in a hurry to land a job, I let myself be convinced prospects for me there were hopeless.

The Sun, Globe, Evening Telegram and *Evening World* in turn declined to avail themselves of my services for improvement or otherwise.

Hy Baggerly of *The Bulletin* had given me a letter to George Hughes, city editor of *The Evening Mail*, but I had held out from using it, because I preferred getting a job on my own merits, if I had any, rather than depending on friendly influence. Now, having made no dent in New York's hard-boiled editorial front, I decided to use Hy's note of introduction. The bankroll of $300, with which I had started out, was slipping fast, and the time was approaching when I should have to visit "Uncle" with a diamond ring and gold watch which Eddie Graney and Morris Levy, California fight promoters, had given to me, and a diamond-studded penknife from Jim Coffroth, another promoter.

George Hughes told me how glad he was to meet me and how sorry there was no opening.

"*The Mail* has the greatest cartoonist in the world — Homer Davenport," he said.

Segment of Swinnerton *Little Tigers* pantomime from a Sunday color page in New York *Journal*. The identity of the characters in the daily panels Swinnerton started in *The Examiner* in 1892 had come from the bruin that is emblazoned on the California State flag. The switch to Little Tigers in New York was actuated by "Father Knickerbocker's" having been superseded as a New York image by the impression made in the "Tammany Tiger" cartoons of Thomas Nast. The latter's work for *Harper's Weekly* had been instrumental in the downfall of William M. Tweed as boss of Tammany Hall.

"Yes, I know you have Homer Davenport, but my work isn't the same as his."

"No doubt you're right on that point," Mr. Hughes agreed; and again I toted my bundle of sample sketches out of a newspaper office.

That night I decided on a new tack. In thinking back over what had happened to me in the New York newspaper offices, I suddenly realized I had not been turned down by sports editors. I had not tried to see any sports editors.

The office boy who halted me at the editorial offices of *The Evening Mail* next morning said:

"Say, you're the boob that was in here yesterday, ain't you?"

I had given thought to my approach. With dignity I agreed I had been there yesterday; that Mr. Hughes was a friend of mine. I now wanted to see the sports editor.

"Take my tip, Jack, and don't butt in on Fred when he's makin' up. He's apt to pi a page form on your conk."

"Fred who?"

"Fred Wenck, the sportin' editor. He's a athalete."

At my insistence the boy reluctantly took my message to the ferocious and athletic Mr. Wenck. He returned in a few moments, told me I was to go in, and muttered: "Don't blame me, Jack; I gave ya plenty a warnin'."

A stocky built, dark-complexioned young chap with the pinkest cheeks I had seen in New York stopped me as I entered the city room.

"You Goldberg? I'm Wenck. Well, whatin-ell do you want?"

"A job. I'm a cartoonist. I've got some samples with me."

"And you've also got just two minutes to show 'em."

Wenck studied them for a much longer time than he had allotted for the inspection.

"They're not as rotten as I thought they'd be," he said at length. "You say you made 'em?" He looked me over as though in doubt. "You're sure you made 'em?"

"Honest, I did."

"Leave 'em here and come back tomorrow morning — but not when I'm making up the sports pages. Get me?"

When I returned next day Wenck told me he had talked it over with the managing editor, whose identity I found to be Theopholus P. Niles.

"How much salary do you want?"

"I don't know. What do you pay?"

"Well, I tried to jimmy $75 a week out of the boss, but the big flounder won't stand for more than fifty smackers. The only person a managing editor wants to get good jack is the managing editor. What about the fifty fish?"

I almost dropped when he mentioned $50 as the salary. I had expected less to start in New York.

"Fifty'll be all right as a starter," I said a little loftily.

"Then consider yourself on the pay roll at a half century per. There's a meeting on of the A.A.U. at Madison Square Garden. Go up there and see what you can dig out of it."

James E. Sullivan and Justice Bartow S. Weeks were the chief officials of the Amateur Athletic Union then. It was Justice Weeks who made this first assignment much easier that it might have been otherwise. He wore whiskers, and they were a godsend to me. I doted on a face covered with quite a crop of these. I had found them extremely helpful in reproducing likenesses. If an artist gets a bewhiskered gentleman's foliage right he doesn't have to fret much about the other details.

Wenck looked at the half-page cartoon I made and said it wasn't as good workmanship as the samples I had shown him. But he used it, and I kept working at *The Mail*. But I was not satisfied with my work. I believed that the public did not like it. And so, for the first time, it became rather hard to work, except when I did it simply for the love of drawing. I knew I was not getting ahead.

One evening a bunch of my friends, who

YOU SEE, IT'S ALL VERY SIMPLE - THE TRANSMISSION TAKES THE CARBURETTER BY THE HAND AND LEADS IT INTO THE CYLINDER WHERE THEY MEET THE DOUBLE IGNITION GOING FOR A STROLL IN THE FLY WHEEL THEREBY BRINGING ABOUT AN INTAKE AROUND TOWARDS THE OUTLET VALVES, ALL OF WHICH CAUSES THE CAR TO MOVE OUT OF THE GARAGE

YOU OUGHT TO GO TO A PAINT SHOP OR A HARDWARE STORE FOR YOUR MEALS

BRING ME A CYLINDER OF TONNEAU PUDDING WITH GASOLINE SAUCE ON THE SIDE

THEY EVEN EAT IN THE CHUG CHUG LANGUAGE.

YOU'RE LUCKY TO REMAIN SANE WHILE LEARNING THE FINE POINTS OF THE GAME.

THAT DEAR OLD TIRE DOESN'T LOOK GOOD FOR MORE THAN 600 MILES AN HOUR-SHE SEEMS A TRIFLE TOO SHY AND BASHFUL

THE MOTORING BUG CONSIDERS EVERY PART OF HIS MACHINE ALMOST HUMAN

VOT ISS DISS - A ZOO?

PAPA, BUY ME THAT TEDDY BEAR

IT WOULDN'T BE SAFE TO WEAR ONE OF THOSE FUR COATS WHERE PRESIDENT ROOSEVELT IS HUNTING.

HAIL! ALL HAIL KING GASOLINE !!

57

were rooting for me sincerely, made a suggestion: they argued that I would stand a much better chance if I changed my name. They almost persuaded me that Americans are so narrow-minded that they are prejudiced against certain names. Their insinuation was that, while I might be all right personally, my name was a bad trademark. "Rube Goldberg" did not sound as musical as "Homer Davenport," or "John Tenniel." I admitted that "mountain of gold" — the meaning of my name — might not exactly describe my financial condition, but I insisted that it was a perfectly good name. Besides, it was my father's name; and he was the one person without whose sympathetic understanding I never would have dared attempt to realize my ambition. I lay awake all night, trying to picture myself named O'Sullivan, or Bridgewater, or something like that. Then I realized that it was idiotic even to consider such a thing; that I would be ashamed of it all the remainder of my life; and that, if a man's achievements are no bigger than the sound of his name, it doesn't much matter what his name may be.

Instead of deciding to use a *nom de plume* I determined to try to add a little to the honor my father and mother had brought to the name. Whether this decision had anything to do with it or not, work immediately became easier and my resolve to succeed greater.

Within three months I was drawing a daily seven-column cartoon which ran across the full width of one sports page. In the three center columns it was deeper than at the two ends, a shape which was useful for make-up purposes, as the center drop kept the headline type from running together. My regular formula was to make a central cartoon, with four smaller pictures around it, two on either side.

It bothered me how I could use the space in that three-column drop to the best advantage. One day I spoke to Franklin P. Adams — F.P.A. — than a humorist columnist of *The Mail,* about it.

I HAVE MET===BY GOLDBERG

THERE WAS A BUMP AT LEAGUE PARK

Al Orth Had His Smile Bumped Off by the Athletics—He Got His, and That's About All There Was to It, See?—But He Was Not the Only One.

By GYM BAGLEY.

It's only those who reach the dizzy heights know what it is to fall.

And there was a bump up at American League park yesterden, the splash of which tore holes in the surrounding scenery and isn't yet done reverberating back from the crags that line the Palisades.

It was awful. It was even worse than that.

Louis Mann said it was really too bad. Big Bill Devery said it was tough. Mike, the Bite said—never mind what Mike said.

When Al Orth stepped forth to the music of the band and took his place at the cross roads of action, little he wotted of his fate. He was smiling as of yore. To him the day was fair and full of promise. No dark clouds were hovering on

there with the cherries. He couldn't stem for a little bit. And the Quakers fell upon him, likewise, and smote him fore and aft and eke amidships and in some other places.

And then Castleton, he of the South wing, relieved Mr. Hughes of all further responsibility. And they smote not Castleton. But he was too late.

It was rough going for pitchers. Dygert, too, who lobbed them over for the Athletics, was severely soaked in the slats of his endeavor and had to give way to his red brother, the Bender Chief.

But don't, for a second, allow these minutes of the meeting ti lead you to believe that the Quakers had any rollers under them, and were going under wraps any part of the way. Nothing like it. The Yanks were giving them a fight all the time.

They made one of their game rallies in

the sixth and seventh innings and began to clout the ball. And you know how they can clout it when they start. But the parting came too late.

It will be the Athletics again this afternoon on the hill.

Tim Hurst umpired on the bases. Tim has been trained down so fine that you could hardly see him from the grand stand.

N. B.—This isn't so, but Tim asked me to get his name in the paper.

* * *

Hal Chase must have been nervous. Was it the Big Raise? It is so seldom that he makes a bum throw that it goes for the Great Surprise.

* * *

And how they did root. When it comes to the noise thing, the mob at American League park has them all hushed to a lullaby.

"Did it ever occur to you," said Adams, "what funny questions people ask? You meet a fellow who's been out of town and say to him 'Hello, you back again?' On an August day, with the thermometer at 100 even, a man is pushing a lawn mower around the front yard and oozing like a sponge, when some nut comes along and asks 'Cutting the grass?'"

Foolish Questions No. 1 appeared in the three-column drop next day. It showed a man who had fallen from the top of the Flatiron Building, at that time the best known skyscraper in New York, and saying to the goofy one who asks if he's hurt: "No, you idiot. I jump off this building every day to limber up for business."

I had no intention of making *Foolish Questions* a regular feature. Its origin was purely accidental, and my idea was to run one whenever I couldn't think of anything else to fill up the three-column drop. But after several of them had appeared I knew they had struck that human note which gets anything of this kind over, whether it is a drawing, a song or a piece of writing. Flocks of letters began coming in, reading: "Dear Rube, here's a funny one for your *Foolish Questions*," and then outlining an idea. Some of the readers of *The Mail* went so far as to telephone me their suggestions.

Within a week I had promoted *Foolish Questions* from the bottom of the daily spread to the more conspicuous position at the right-hand side. Fred Wenck, feeling a personal responsibility for me, seemed especially tickled about the good break. In less than two weeks from the day the first *Foolish Questions* appeared, he asked me how I'd like to sign a contract for the remaining nine months of the year.

"The big noise" — meaning Niles — "has loosened up enough to give you sixty-five dollars a week for the next six months and seventy-five dollars for the following three months. I wanted to make it seventy-five dollars and one hundred dollars, but there never was an M.E. with any sense. Some day the ideal newspaper will be

published without a managing editor."

This salary jump was so unexpected I began wondering whether the reason for it didn't mean people there had gone daffy. *The Mail* had some real Names working for it — F.P.A., Grantland Rice, O. O. McIntyre and others. It seemed to me just a question of when the day of reckoning would come and we should all wake up in the psychopathic ward at Bellevue — Wenck, Niles, I, and everybody else who was in any way *particeps criminis* to the swindle.

After *Foolish Questions* had been running several years, readers of *The Mail* began to show less enthusiasm about writing and telephoning in suggestions for it and I sensed that it was up to me to get something new in my daily cartoon spread to attract responses. But what? I pieced together a hundred different catch phrases without hitting on one which seemed to have the essential human note. No matter where I was or what I was doing, the thought beset me: "Where am I going to get that gag to pinch-hit for *Foolish Questions*?" Meeting people had a new significance; maybe there would be something in their get-up or facial expression or conversation which would give me the desperately needed hint. Somewhere, somehow, and pretty darn quick I had to catch up with a regular idea.

One evening I dropped in to see the vaude-ville show on the old Hammerstein Roof, which was one of the most popular amusement places in the New York White Way district at that time. One act followed another, but as for their meaning anything to me I might as well have been sitting on the Battery sea wall. It was not until some comic repartee excited me that I sat up and took notice. What had caught my atten-tion was a line running, "I'm the guy that put the salt in the ocean." For the first three words of that inspired sentence I inwardly uttered three cheers. They were exactly what I needed to round out an idea which had been struggling painfully to break through the bony structure surmounting my neck.

As a sidelight in the daily cartoon I had created the character of a grotesque little man,

who was always shown in some unexpected place — coming out of a flowerpot, sitting on a chandelier, or riding a bicycle upside down on the ceiling, and so on, while making some sort of a wise crack apropos of conversation being carried on by central figures in the cartoon. Readers of *The Mail* and other papers* then

publishing my cartoons had indicated more than a passing interest in him, and it had been in my mind that he could be developed into something more than a minor feature. Now I had found the way to accomplish this. Henceforth he would be the hero of a series called *I'm the Guy.*

*Frank Parker Stockbridge, reminiscing in *The American Press*, May 1931, recalled that when he became Managing Editor of *The Evening Mail* in 1915, "the star feature controlled by this New York daily was Rube Goldberg. He was getting a salary of $25,000 a year. His daily comic strip was being sold for us by the Mc-Clure Newspaper Syndicate and was grossing about $24,000 a year, so that Goldberg was costing *The Mail* about $1,000 plus the McClure commission of ten percent.

"So we were getting Goldberg very cheap. He had arrived at a point of popularity in which his only possible rivals were Bud Fisher and George McManus. In my judgment, his work at that time was far superior in subtlety and imaginative quality to either *Mutt and Jeff* or *Bringing Up Father.* I regarded Goldberg then, as I do now, as having the keenest and most brilliant mind of any of the comic artists, while he was far more industrious and reliable than some of the others.

"Rube and I got to be good friends, so that I was somewhat surprised when he came into my office one day late in 1915 and said:

" 'Boss, I hate to leave you, but I don't see how I can stay on *The Mail* any longer. My contract expires at the end of the year, and I have got a big offer from Hearst.'

" 'Don't be foolish,' I replied. 'You say that you hate to leave us, yet you talk about quitting as if it were a certainty. Would you rather stay here?'

" 'Why, of course, I would much rather stay with *The Mail*,' said Goldberg, 'but I don't see how I can turn down $50,000 a year.'

" 'Who said anything about turning it down?' I countered. I was satisfied that we could make as much money syndicating Goldberg as Hearst could.

"It took some arguing to get the necessary authority to sign a new contract with Goldberg, but I succeeded."

Mr. Stockbridge had become favorably impressed with Virgil V. McNitt, a former *Cleveland Press* editor who had established a syndicate called Central Press Association, and called him to New York.

" 'We want to start the Evening Mail Syndicate,' I told him, 'with you as manager. Your brother can run your Central Press out in Cleveland for a while, and we will pay you a salary and percentage.'

"He jumped on the cars and went to Chicago to see Victor Lawson at *The Daily News.* The next morning I had a wire from McNitt saying that he had closed with *The Daily News*, then started out after the other old customers and new ones. As I recollect it, before our new contract with Goldberg went into effect, McNitt had sold him for more than the guarantee.

"In 1918, a year and a half after I had left *The Evening Mail*, control of the paper passed to Henry L. Stoddard, but Virgil McNitt negotiated a deal whereby he took over the Evening Mail Syndicate."

The association of Goldberg with McMitt and the latter's partner, Charles McAdam, in what became McNaught Syndicate, was to continue many years. Rube was also to be a feature of Hearst newspapers while with McNitt and McAdam.   — C. K.

The idea I sought to express in *I'm the Guy* was that no matter how much we marvel at the miracles performed by science, the everyday mysteries of life are still perplexing. Why does Swiss cheese have holes? Why do grapes have seeds, dogs have tails, trees have leaves, bulls have horns? Let us say the subject was fish. The first three panels of the cartoon would show a fisherman much elated over making a fine haul and then getting a bone in his throat when he sat down to enjoy the feast. In the final panel the little old man would appear in some impossible position and, in response to the question "Who are you?", he would say "I'm the guy that put the bones in fish."

I'm the Guy caught on with the public. But it had one weakness I had not foreseen, which was that there were not enough of these miracles to keep it going indefinitely. I got around this by making the final punch a play on words, instead of building the incident around some freak of nature. For example, a writer could be shown in the third floor back of a Greenwich Village boarding house, filling reams of manuscript and cursing fate because he had to use so much expensive ink. The old fellow would drop in and announce that he was the guy who put the ink in think. Or in other situations, he could put the con in conference, the rush in Russia, the sip in Mississippi or the pain in paint. What I could or couldn't make him do depended entirely on how complete a dictionary I had; and I at once saw to it that the one my reference library contained was the biggest and wordiest the market offered. Later I wrote the verses of a popular song, *I'm the Guy*. (Burt Grant composed the music.)

It was not my only song.

3

Foolish Questions

Among other questionable ponderables in the series, not illustrated here, and the responses:

Why, Dearie, did you get wet?
Of course not — the rain is dry today.

Are you going in swimming?
No — I'm on my way to the blacksmith shop to get some dill pickles.

John, have you been drinking?
Just a slight attack of nervousness, m'Dearie.

Willie, have you been playing football again?
No, Father. I've been out picking bananas off an egg plant.

Hello, Bill, gettin' a shine?
No — I'm painting a portrait of a string bean.

Why, hello, Jones — are you still in town?

No — I'm touring Europe in a wheelbarrow.

Having a little game of billiards?
No — I'm cooking a Spanish omelet.

Hello, young man — are you sick?
No — I feel so good I have to stay in bed to keep myself from pushing over the Brooklyn Bridge.

Good morning, Jones, are you shaving?
No, you boob — I'm peeling potatoes.

Young man, did you fall?
No — I'm taking a little nap.

My gracious, Bud. Have you been arrested again?
No, Maggie, I'm in here rehearsing a troupe of trained oysters for a marathon race.

Hello, girls, are you taking a little bite to eat?

No — we're taking a horseback ride in the subway.

Anthony, are you smoking again?
No, Cleopatra — I'm taking a bath in a bowl of clam chowder.

Waterin' the lawn, Si?
No — I'm harnessing up my automobile for a drive on the lake.

Hector, are you tired?
No, dearie — I'm taking a lesson in physical culture.

Morning, Judge — taking a bath?
No, you mutt. I'm shoveling the snow off the roof with a teaspoon.

Reading a book, Henry?
No — I'm playing a violin solo on a base drum.

Fixing your machine, Partner?
No, you dip — I'm writing a poem about the beauty of a dog biscuit.

Morning, Children — playing marbles?
No, you old mummy — we're studying Greek in a Chinese laundry.

Are you typewriting something, Sadie?
No, Jean — I'm picking wild flowers in a livery stable.

Hello, Boys — doing a little boxing?
No — we're having a swimming race on the boardwalk.

Young man, are you kissing my daughter?
No, Madam — I'm shampooing her hair with a bottle of furniture polish.

Fishing, Hank?
No — I'm out yachting in a milk wagon.

Is that kid crying again?
No, you nut — he's singing a grand opera selection in rag-time.

My Son, my Son, what are you doing?
Can't you see I'm out in the hothouse picking erasers off the rubber plant!

Are you busy?
No — I'm just loafing around here answering foolish questions.

Hello, Jim, got a dog?
No, you dope — this is a Norwegian gold fish.

FOOLISH QUESTIONS-NO.1,071

4

From The Mail

This could be called one of my earliest "invention" cartoons; in *The Evening Mail* soon after my advent in New York City resulted in my having top space daily in sporting pages. What impresses me more, looking back now, is that soon after my arrival in New York, *I* was a by-liner (see the story in the two right-hand columns) in a New York paper as a *writer!*

I have submitted tolerantly, in gentlemanly fashion, to the editor's idea that other of my early cartoons in *The Evening Mail* that follow also are of interest, if not of historic significance.

● An early cartoon in *The Evening Mail* went this way: A fresh-air fiend opened a window, with the result that his pet owl sneezed into a toy bugle. The toot summoned National Guardsmen who collided with a milkman and broke his bottles. The spilled milk attracted a swarm of cats, and their yowling woke up the neighbors. A political candidate, mistaking the neighbors' yells at the cats for pleas that he save the country, popped his night-shirted torso out of a window and made an acceptance speech.

The title was "Device for Nominating a Candidate for High Office."

70

INVENTIONS FOR SPORTS—BY GOLDBERG.

I PASSED UP A $100,000 OFFER FOR MY NEW PLAY

WHEN I MANAGED JIM CORBETT, WE WOULDN'T ENTER THE RING FOR ANYTHING LESS THAN A MILLION

PARASOL ATTACHMENTS FOR SIDEWALK PERFORMERS

THE VIBRATORY SPRINKLING CAN FOR THOROUGHBREDS

THIS MOUNTAIN AIR IS GREAT

INTO HIS FRIED LIVER AND ONIONS, KID!

FOR THOSE WHO ARE NOT THERE WITH THE PRICE OF A VACATION - A COOL SUMMER LANDSCAPE TO BE HUNG IN THE BEDROOM WHERE IT CAN BE SEEN EVERY MORNING UPON AWAKENING.

THE HUMAN ICE CREAM FREEZER IS ALWAYS REFRESHING.

FIGHT-GOERS SHOULD WEAR THE ELECTRIC-FAN-DRY-BATTERY-HEAD-GEAR — VERY COOLING.

HUMID WEATHER CANNOT FEAZE THE SPORTING GEE

Old Sol's Rays May Be Working Overtime, but the Baseball and Fight Fans Never Will Welsh on the Show.

By R. L. GOLDBERG.

If to-morrow was election day and the iceman ran for President he would be elected by acclamation. As the thermometer dances the can-can to Old Sol's latest tune, the vender of the solidified sparkling nectar continues to gain in popularity. Every time he sells a pound of his goods he lets loose another verse of "How would you like to be me?" and we answer back in accents streaming with perspiration, "Take every cent we've got (goodness gracious, ain't it hot!) give us ice, ice, ice; give us ice at any price; keep us cool!"

Four hundred thousand people may have gone to the country. But the crowds at the ball grounds haven't diminished. The mobs at the tracks are as big as ever. The fights are patronized as well as ever. The streets are as crowded as ever. Which all shows that an elephant with a hair cut looks as big as ever.

the entire limelight. Nelson is now in San Francisco training.

Philadelphia Jack O'Brien has taken up bowling. We shall not be surprised if we hear that the proprietor of the place where Jack bowls comes down to work some fine morning and finds one of his alleys missing.

H. L. Baggerly, the Frisco sporting authority who secured O'Brien's confession in full, is here in New York, and says that the Quaker salve artist is losing money on his new St. James hotel on the coast. Sorry, Jack, but we can't give you a benefit. You have all our loose change already.

SUMMERS AND ERNE IN PHILA.

Philadelphia, June 19.—A bout of inter-

FIGHT FANS SEE THE REAL THING AT BILLY ELMER'S ROOF GARDEN

While Cooled by Breezes Enjoyed Two Knockouts Within Four Rounds.

By GYM BAGLEY.

when you can get two knockouts in- of four rounds and a hurrying, rat-

was their last fight on earth, and they wanted to roll across Jordan's final tide with a clear record.

In the third round Jack got to Eddie with a short right hook to the chops and Eddie took to the floor. He struggled game'y to his prone only to meet another

Then Stacked Up Against a Six-Round Go That Kept Them Yelling.

my word with the members. Next Tuesday Andy McGarry and Charley Seiger

You can find here that in 1907 the New York American League team was referred to, during a transitional period, as both "Highlanders" and "Yankees." One good thing about these old cartoons from the sports pages: they cater to nostalgia, with their mentions of relatively peaceful heroes of yesteryears.

E MET---BY GOLDBERG.

GRIFF PILING IT UP ON THE TIGERS

While Highlanders Sit Gloating Over Their Two Straight Victories Over Detroit, the Michigan Fans Are Sleeped in Gloom.

Detroit, Mich., Aug. 17.—There is only one bright spot here to-day; only a small crowd cares whether the sun shines or not. And that's the Euclid hotel, where the Yankees are stopping during their stay here, and the Highlanders themselves. Around the Tiger camp a deep gloom has settled and the local fans are tired.

Thursday morning the Michiganders neglected business to tell each other of great times to come. There never was other, making all kinds of hair-raising stops, and more than tha., of all his throws to first or anywhere else not one could be criticised. He's the real Kid Elberfeld again.

While the Tigers succeeded in getting men on base in every inning but one they were never really dangerous until toward the end. Then Hogg weakened. In the eighth he passed two and gave a pair of hits—this was the first inning by the way in which Detroit managed to

BIG BOWERMAN FITS WELL ON FIRST BAG

Michigander Has Developed the First Base Habit and Now He Wants to Play at the First Station.

By GYM BAGLEY.

And the final game of the series below the series

IF PLAYS WERE ONLY TRUE TO LIFE--

BAGLEY TELLS ABOUT A FUNNY BALL GAME

If You Don't Believe That There Was a ½ to 0 Contest Read This Diagnosis of a Ball That Parted in the Middle.

By GYM BAGLEY.

A boob from the Bronx, who thinks he's funny, writes me asking about a game where the score was ½ to 0.

But whether this boob knows it or not, there was such a game, and Rowdy Jack O'Connor, now playing with the St. Louis Browns, was the guy who made the half run.

Edward Everett Bell, Ben Moses and George Grant saw the game, and can testify to the accuracy of the following account; that is, its accuracy in the main. It is some time now since I saw the play, and, while the principal action is fresh in my thinkery, I may go a bit

pitcher wasted one, but Jack didn't bite. Then he picked out a fast high one, and that ball started on the most memorable journey that ever happened in the history of baseball.

Jack hit it so hard that it split in two of the evenest halves that is. They collected them afterward and they weighed exactly alike, to the fraction of a drachm. I know, for it was I who weighed them in the drug store on the corner.

One half went sailing over the center field fence. It kept the round side fore-most. The other half had its flat side to the wind and that put a crimp in its

TALENT FORGET THEIR TROUBLES

74

BY GOLDBERG.

IN REAL LIFE

GIBLETT GETS GROGGY FROM THE CHLOROFORM - THE MANAGER OF THE TEAM THINKS HE IS DRUNK AND FIRES HIM - BADEGG KILLS OLD MAN BLOSSOM AND MARRIES MAGNOLIA - WHEN HE TRIES TO COLLECT THE $100,000 INSURANCE, HE FINDS THAT THE IN-SURANCE COMPANY HAS JUST FAILED FOR TWO CENTS ON THE DOLLAR - MAGNOLIA GETS A DIVORCE AND GOES ON THE STAGE - BADEGG BECOMES A SECOND-STORY WORKER AND GIBLETT GETS A JOB AS A DUMMY IN A CLOTHING STORE CURTAIN

WHY CAN'T THEY FIX PLAYS IN REAL WAY?

Then, Maybe, the Yankess Would Win a Pennant and the Other Clubs Would Have to Beat It Back to the Bush.

By R. L. GOLDBERG.

If a playright ever attempted to create a production on a real life-like basis, the audience would rise up en masse and lynch him on the spot. The hero's career would be so full of knots and kinks and other undesirable rough places that a street-paving squad would have to be called in to flatten it out with a steam-roller.

The stage generally shuffles the good things into the palm of the deserving party, while the dealer in low-down stuff is brought to the bar of justice and given anywhere from 10 to 100 years' hard labor. In real life the villain is brought to the bar of a first-class cafe and given anywhere from 50 to 10,000 drinks.

If a play were to be written around the checkered career of the Yanks, we would probably see Jack Chesbro or some other slab artist pluck a game out of the very grasp of Defeat, win the girl and put the team at the head of the league. The Chicagos and Detroits and several dozen other teams that are now ahead of the Yankees in the race for the pennant would be relegated to the bush league and their respective managers given long terms of imprisonment on general principles. The atmosphere would be filled with chicken gravy.

But in real cold, hard, cruel, wicked life—yoi, yoi, it's awful! The star pitcher goes in to save the game and comes out looking like a tramp who had just been hit by a battleship. The faithful rooters go out to the ball grounds and roof themselves blue in the face only to see the home team ground into a jar of orange marmalade—and a small jar at that. Clark Griffith stays awake all night doping out the road to victory, and wakes up the next morning with a taste in his mouth like a pair of old tan shoes and a pay roll in front of him as long as the fine imposed upon the Standard Oil.

Why can't we arrange things in real life like authors do in plays? Why? Because we have no control over the movements of the scene shifters.

M'GRAW'S BUNCH IS IN NEED OF REPAIRS

STANDING OF THE CLUBS.

AMERICAN LEAGUE.							NATIONAL LEAGUE.						
Club.	W.	L.	P.C.	Club.	W.	L.	P.C.	Club.	W.	L.	P.C.	Club.	W.	L.	P.C.
Detroit	57	36	.613	New York	44	51	.463	Chicago	72	26	.735	Brooklyn	44	54	.449
Chicago	60	39	.606	Boston	39	55	.415	Pittsburg	57	34	.613	Cincinnati	44	54	.449
Phila	57	37	.606	St. Louis	31	56	.411	New York	55	39	.585	Boston	38	57	.400
Cleveland	55	43	.514	Washing'n	29	63	.315	Phila	51	40	.507	St. Louis	23	78	.228

RESULTS OF YESTERDAY'S GAMES.

St. Louis, 8; New York, 4.
Boston, 2; Chicago, 1.
Philadelphia, 4; Detroit, 2.
Washington, 7; Cleveland, 2.

Brooklyn, 4; Cincinnati 2.
Philadelphia, 5; Chicago, 6.
New York-Pittsburg and St. Louis-Boston games postponed. Rain.

GAMES SCHEDULED FOR TO-DAY.

St. Louis at New York.
Cleveland at Washington.
Chicago at Philadelphia.
Detroit at Philadelphia.

New York at Pittsburg.
Brooklyn at Cincinnati.
Philadelphia at Chicago.
Boston at St. Louis.

BAGLEY DISCOVERS A NEW CHAMP.

Who Wants to Fight Any of Them, White, Black, Brown or Yellow, and Don't Care for Gate Receipts, but When the "John Smith" Yanks $10,000 Out of His Jeans the Dreamer Awakes.

By GYM BAGLEY.

Did you ever cop the upstairs rattler at Park place, Bo, after you had been adding a little more to what you had and only waited for the other gazoosh to get through his story so that you could tell yours? And you were headed straight for Ninety-third street and the little home comforts and the Other Things that were coming to you on the side because everything was cold but the ice water. And when Ninety-third street was made and the guard guy called out something that sounded like a Jack O'Brien excuse, and you passed it up with the contempt it deserved and slept peacefully on like a babe who had never known a patent food until they put you off at the last station. And then when you woke up again, you were at the Battery. And when you had coughed up all your nickels trying to break off in the middle of the line, you waited in the early dawn for Ninety-third street to come around to you.

Did you ever do all that, Bo? Well—but what's this got to do with the New Challenger?

I saw him first, in a strange nimbus that I hadn't piped since the days of John L. and Jack Dempsey. He edged in with a certain air of modesty, even

unloading his bonnet, and asked, in a Well Modulated voice, if he could say a word.

I told him to go as far as he liked. The cover looked good to me and I wanted a peek inside.

"I'm after the pugilistic championship of the world," he said. I don't know whether I can cop, but I'm willing and anxious to try."

This began all right and I asked his name.

"John Smith," he replied. "I'm twenty-one, weigh 190 pounds, five feet, eleven inches tall and I have learned to box."

"You look like a strong young fellow and you haven't the face of a quitter. But a 'John Smith' can't fight. You'll have to change it to Burns or O'Brien or something like that."

"John Smith is my name," he came back, quietly, but with decision. "I fight as John Smith or I don't fight at all."

"Well, you'll have to go in green tights, anyway."

He didn't seem to quite get this and looked puzzled. He certainly was innocent. I couldn't help thinking that perhaps he was brought up in Tom O'Rourke's stable.

"I'll fight any man in the world," he went on, "from Joe Grim up to Jim Jeffries. I don't draw any color line, black, brown, yellow or blue. I don't want the big ones till I have disposed of the others. I'll take them all on, one at a time, until I'm stopped, and then I'll quit and go back to my business of teaching school."

"But you haven't any rep." I broke in. I never heard of you. You can't expect the high lights of this noble profession to consider an unknown like you."

"They all had to begin some time, didn't they?" he retorted.

I was going to say that while this looked like a self-evident proposition, most of them nowadays were ready-made. And some of them made over. But I only nodded.

He went on: "I haven't heard of any of them that were in the game for the good of their health or in order to please mother. I realize that I won't draw in the go-off, but they will. Any one I don't stop inside the limit can have the whole gate. I don't want any special arrangement. I don't want a cent if I don't win. And by winning, I don't mean a decision on points. Any time I fail to knock my man out before the last round is reached, I will consider myself defeated."

I looked at this startler in speechless surprise.

"The gate doesn't count with me at that," he continued, "until I have shown that I belong in the candidate class."

He ducked down in his jeans and pulled up a bundle that would scare off a run on a bank.

"There's $10,000 in money," he said,

TIGERS OFF FOR ITHACA.

Princeton Team and Its Rooters Passed Through Here This Morn

----By R. L. Goldberg.

T-DONOVAN
SLOW DRAW

1, Oct 25 —More than
saw Joe Walcott and
clinch and hug through
ds at the Standard Ath-
Lymansville last night
ght hard enough to get
half the spectators left
twelve rounds had been
e damaging blow was
e fight, Walcott missing
of the time and Dono-
he without a wallop that
ded a bantam.

MS WAS
FOR BONNER

et 25 —Art Simms put
against Jim Bonner, a
one-time slasher, Jack
nt at the Broadway Ath-
w needed in lasting but

POOR RIDE BEAT LAWRENCE P. DALEY.

The Cook Horse Was Pounds the Best in the Opening Event, but Under the Hauling About He Received from Jockey Nicol the Best He Could Do Was to Finish Second.

By "TOMMY" TOMPKINS.

There was some good racing at Jamaica yesterday and some bad. The former, however, so far predominated that on the way home the talent completely forgot that they had seen a race or two that very properly could have been inquired into by the stewards.

Take that ride that Nicol put up on Lawrence P. Daley in the first event, for instance. Wasn't it about as crude an effort as could have been expected from a boy that never had seen a race track?

There is no question as to the Cook horse being the class of the race, and at first clos estudents of form were inclined to back him. It did not take them long, however, to discover that the proper money was not showing on the began to why. In main

It wasn't a pleasant sight for his backers, what few he had, and they were not chary about their comments.

Finally, in the stretch, when The Squire had a lead that even Colin could not have overcome, Nicol steered Daley clear of interference and then and there he proved that with equal handling he could have run over the top of The Squire. He closed on the outside, going two strides to the leader's one, and at the end all but caught him.

Of course all this does not mean that there was anything criminal about Nicol's ride, but it certainly was an incompetent one. If he had been as alert at the post as was Miller, Daley would have won by a good margin of day light, and a lot of un been

The worst thing about the whole affair was that the kind of a race that Daley ran was plainly indicated in the ring before the horses went to the post.

Outside of that one race there wasn't much to find fault with. True Brussell made a botch of his ride on Royal Lady in the second race, but he is hardly to be blamed. Every one knows that he is not a first class jockey and racegoers have ceased to expect first class work from him. Any man that bets on him is taking a chance and knows it.

Royal Lady was the best horse and should have won. Brussell did his best and was riding like a demon, a very mild one it is true, in the stretch, but young Guy Burns on Marster always held him

THE CANDY KID—

TALENT HAVE THE LAYERS ON THE RUN

At Least the Men Who Do the Guessing Get a Good Break, and Before the Day Is Over They Take Many Thousands of Dollars from the Men in the Ring.

By "TOMMY" TOMPKINS.

While no great wave of excitement swept over Belmont park yesterday, there was enough doing throughout the day to keep all hands pleasantly engaged; that is, all hands except the gentlemen in the ring, who now call themselves layers, but in the old days were proud to be known as bookmakers. They were engaged all right, but it hardly could be called pleasantly so, for their activity consisted principally in paying out money to the thousands who seemed unable to land on the loser.

The rout of the ring, that's what it really was, started in the very first race. True, some money was lost on Samuel H. Harris, who had a fit of the slows

horse as is the one named after Terry McGovern's old manager.

At that those who cashed were lucky, for the way the race was run Yada seemed to be the best horse. The latter was in close quarters all during the latter part of the race and never really had a chance to do justice to himself.

In the second race the talent got there with the entire bank roll. Try as they would the layers could not give anything away except Frank Farrell's Wave Crest. The public simply wouldn't have anything else, and as Wave Crest won easily the ring lost heavily despite the short odds.

Lane Allen made good for favorite players in the third race despite his 124 pounds. It was a handicap, and such a

was nothing left to give Lane Allen an argument, and when he came home alone the layers found themselves many thousands of dollars poorer.

While the victory of Uncle in the fourth race did not hurt the ring, his price being too short for the average player, Lawrence P. Daley's second did put a crimp in many a bank roll. The Cook horse was second choice in the betting, and as there always was even money, or at the least 4 to 5, against him a place, that is where most of the public money went.

The one ray of light that penetrated the layers' gloom came in the fifth race. Despite the outrageous weight of 139 pounds, Brookdale Nymph was made the favorite and was heavily

RICE WINS P[...]
BOUT WITH [...]

Mount Vernon, Oct. 10.—
New London, Conn., east[...]
cision over Spike Robison [...]
in a private fight pulled [...]
Fellows' clubhouse yeste[...]
finish Robison was so muc[...]
wear that he almost colla[...]
be helped to his dressing [...]
was game and took all [...]
Rice could give him, b[...]
punches to the kidneys [...]
and in another round the [...]
fighter would have won [...]

YOUNG KENN[...]
MATTY B[...]

Johnny Willis, matchma[...]
tional Athletic club a[...]

3.   4.

JOHNSON NOT YET RIPE TO BE OUSTED.

Comiskey Must Wait a Bit Before He Can Bring About Downfall of American League Leader.

So Ban Johnson is being hunted by the man with the hook. That's what our neighbors tell us, and it's probably true. But this is not exactly news. Johnson's scalp has been sought on other occasions, still they went ahead and boosted his salary, as director-general of the American league, to $10,000 per annum. But we guess that Johnson is too strongly intrenched to be reached at this time.

Charley Comiskey is the magnate who has thrown down the gauntlet to chubby Ban. The Roman says Johnson must go, just the same as the Tammany enemies say Murphy must go. But the derrick has not yet been built that will lift Johnson out of his soft berth. The Johnson-Comiskey feud is nothing new. It was very bitter two years ago, but later Johnson and the Roman shook hands and called the bout a draw. But Comiskey is sore this time. He is accusing Johnson of everything that is detrimental to the American league, and the White Sox principally.

But to Johnson. There are a whole lot of things that Comiskey is saying and has said about Johnson that are worthy of notice. There is no gainsaying the fact that Johnson put the American league where it is to-day. But it is also true that Johnson has run the American league almost as he pleased. This is particularly true where deals for players were concerned. Johnson has often taken it upon himself to ...

By the SPORTING EDITOR.

is to battle Gunner Moir for the alleged world's heavyweight title. Too bad Moir is not good enough to show up the champion sidestepper of pugilism.

If Kid McCoy's racing luck doesn't change soon the Kid will enter the fighting game again. He often feels inclined to take a punch at some of the bookmakers who are getting his bankroll.

Joe Jennette is still without work. The dinge gets the go-by from all the good fighters, and we are beginning to believe that he is feared by some of the alleged fraternity. Jeanette's latest defi is aimed at every fighter in the world. What Jennette should do is to purchase a freight ticket and hike for England. They gave Langford lots of work on the other side, and Joe ought to make good if Langford did.

Lewis (Kid) Goodman is squandering money on postage and ink again. Oh, yes, Goodman is a wrestler. He uses ink when he writes his press notices because he says all good wrestlers write with ink. Here, appended, is Goodwin's most recent spasm:

Lewis (Kid) Goodman the featherweight champion wrestler is to make his last appearance as a wrestler and will meet Albert Gotch in a contest to a finish the latter part of November in this city the reason why is because I am ...

Bookmakers May Drive Kid McCoy Into the Fighting Business Again—Knocks and Boosts.

now a manager of a half dozen first class fighters I was going to leave for England to wrestle all comers with Tom O'Rourke but Mr O'Rourke gave me a tip that if he does good business out their with Joe Rodgers then he will send for me but I think if you cant make no living in this wide America you cannot make it elsewhere.

The Kid appears to be a bit of a philosopher, too. But—well, let this be the Kid's obituary as a press agent. Hope he will be able to make a living in "this wide America."

CINCH BET FOR A.

To decide a bet will you kindly answer the following question:
A bets Chicago Americans were the world's champions up to October 11, 1907.
B bets Detroits were the world's champions up to October 11, 1907. Who wins, A or B?
J. M. COYNE.

FIFTY-MILE RUN FOR BIKERS.

A fifty-mile run into Long Island from Bedford Rest, Brooklyn, to-morrow, will be the closing outdoor event for the year of the Century Road Club of America. More than 100 amateur cyclists have entered, and prizes have been offered for those who finish in good time. It is planned that the party of riders will reach Manhasset in time to witness the hill-climbing contest of the Empire City wheelmen.

GRAND STADIUM FOR OLYMPICS.

Most Complete Athletic Field in the World Being Made Ready for Games in London Next Y...

TE
SON

Rice, of
1 a de-
w York,
he Odd
At the
orse for
had to
Robison
shment
's hard
down.
London
ockout.

'S.
WIN

the Na-

BAGLEY PICKS CUBS TO WIN THE TITLE.

He Bases His Prediction on Baseball Form, if That Counts for Anything—Some People Believe the Fast Pace Set by the Tigers Recently Will Militate Against Them.

By GYM BAGLEY.

Now that the pennant has been won in both the National and the American leagues, all the fanning is directed to which of the respective teams will cop the world's championship.

Taking it right off the roll, it looks like Chicago. On form the Cubs have the popular call on the Tigers. And if you're going to dope a winner, what have you got to go by but form?

All of the gees who know baseball,

The only test of better or worse is the result. You may edge in luck, accident, anything you please, but the runs at the finish of the battle tell the only tale.

When you come to compare the tried veterans of two seasons, the team which has won out in the major league, and made a runaway race of it at that, with a bunch never seriously considered until the tail end of this year, it looks like a soft spot for the vets.

The anxiety and nervous tension must have told on them. The Cubs have had a pink tea in their league. They just ambled home and are fresh, without any scars of conflict. It's like putting a spent runner against one who has just come to the scratch.

Says B: That's no handicap for the Tigers. It's all to their advantage. They are strung to the proper pitch. They're on edge. The Cubs, by reason

KID — By R. L. Goldberg.

DON CREOLE TAPPED THE "BOOKIES."

Con Leighton and His Friends Had Him for a Good Thing, and the Clean-Up Was Enough to Last All Winter—Waited a Long Time to Get a Price, and Now They Have Money to Burn.

By "TOMMY" TOMPKINS.

When Don Creole galloped home an easy winner in the fourth race at the Brighton track yesterday, one of the most carefully planned coups of the year was brought to a successful conclusion.

Don Creole belongs to "Mr. Earle" and is trained by Con Leighton, one of the best of the old school of trainers. He it was who used to handle the horses the late Congressman W. L. Scott

handling one or two and taking down a purse or two just to pay expenses.

Early this year he got Don Creole in his stable and soon found that he had a horse that was one of the greatest mud runners he ever had handled. The horse also had speed, and Con decided to make a killing with him. He had him all readied up at Belmont park in the spring for a maiden race and expected to get all sorts of price about him.

field made him the outsider in the betting, at twelves.

It was just play for him to win, and while he was turning the trick Con and all his friends were laughing themselves to death. When the barrier was released he went with the leader, Arimo, for a little more than half a mile. The latter had enough then, and Don Creole, going to the front, galloped all the rest of the way and came home himself

IF PLAYS WERE ONL

BUTLER WINS WHAT HE COULD HAVE HAD FOR THE ASKING

The Jockey Club Is Willing to Approve His Meeting at the Empire City Course, but Never Has Been Requested To.

By "TOMMY" TOMPKINS.

While Mr. James Butler has not by any means "won a victory" over the Jockey Club, as many put it, he has obtained the right to hold a meeting at there is no reason why Mr. Butler should not go ahead and have a fairly good meeting at his track while the big purses are being fought for at Saratoga. Of course it will not be a first-class meeting

TRUE TO LIFE---BY GOLDBERG.

LUNATICS I HAVE MET--

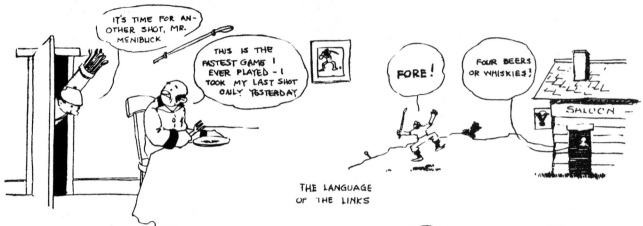

THE LANGUAGE OF THE LINKS

THERE IS ABOUT THREE DAYS INTER- MISSION BETWEEN EACH SHOT

SLOW BASEBALL IS HARD ON THE NERVES

So the Local Fans Are Thankful That There Is No Game Scheduled on the Hill for This Afternoon.

By GYM BAGLEY.

Little old New York will have to do without baseball to-day. The Yanks are on their way to the enemy's country, and the Giants will not butt in on their own historic hollow until to-morrow.

But for all that, the burg may be able to get along without a game after the dose they got up at American League park Saturday. A double header is always a feast, and being a bargain, two sessions for one price, helps its pop.

Still, over five hours of ball—and such ball—instead of being a joy, almost gets to be a pain.

There is no reason for it. Silk O'Loughlin does his best to get the players pp to the bat and keep the game moving, but the players pay as much attention to him as if he were trying to borrow money.

When a guy is playing first base and it takes him fully five minutes to walk from that corner to the plate, he is moving fast—if you don't care how you tell it.

And the pitchers—you'd think they were having their picture took every time they wind up to lob a ball over.

Of course these bunches of scintillating brilliance, who are so deeply imbedded

a close race as a Giant rooter and has had many any auto tour in company with John T. Brush, tells a good one on himself when he was pinched for fast driving in Margaretsburg—wherever that is.

Frankie, accompanied by Mrs. Dwyer, was returning from Canada, where he is heavily interested in Cobalt, Ville Marie and Pontonac mines. Coming through Margaretsburg he ran into the sheriff. The sheriff is like the farmhand whose boss always chased him out to amputate a cord of wood while he was doing nothing—he fills other jobs besides his regular one.

He is not only the sheriff, but the court and the local barber. While he was waiting to be tried by the court on complaint of the sheriff, Frankie thought he needed a shave so that he could present a respectable appearance before the judge. The barber agreed with him that it wouldn't be a bad scheme.

Frankie was shaved, paid his 10 cents for it and was then fined $15.05.

"What's the nickel for?" asked Frankie.

"You didn't tip me," replied the barber, "so I added it to the fine."

HE WILL NOT WALK A BLOCK IN TOWN BUT ON THE LINKS DISTANCE IS NO OBJECT

GIANTS WILL BE ON THE JOB TO-MORROW

After To-Day's Session in the Smoky Burg the McGrawites Will Come Back to Us for the Month's Session.

Pittsburg, Aug. 12.—After the game this afternoon the Giants will pack grips and hike back to good old New York. It was a pretty rocky trip for the McGrawites, still they did better than when

will have an opportunity to get a comfortable lead over the Pittsburgs. This they must do, as they McGrawites finish away from home this year.

To-morrow the Giants will open a series with the Reds. Then will come

-BY GOLDBERG.

THIS PAPER WILL NOT
COUNTENANCE BAD LANGUAGE
SO WE LEAVE THE GENTLE-
MAN'S SPEECH TO
YOUR IMAGINATION

GOLF BUG HARMLESS

By R. L. GOLDBERG.

Our private lunatic asylum is becoming so overcrowded we will soon have to put up a tent in the editorial rooms to make room for the new arrivals. The latest acquisition to the dippy rendezvous is the gentleman who makes a specialty of walloping a poor, innocent little ball all over every inch of a thousand-acre lot—the Knight of the Niblick.

The fact that it takes from three to six months to play a single game of golf makes the so-called leisure class a very easy mark for the attacks of the malady. John D. Rockefeler, Andrew Carnegie and Kid Broad, for this reason, are the prize inmates of this particular ward. When John isn't in his gymnasium hoisting up the price of oil he can be found

LOON XVIII
THE GOLF NUT.

85

JOE HUMPHREYS SOLVES THE MYSTERY OF POLO GROUNDS

In the Guessing Contest as to Who Roasted Doyle Before He Won a Game for the Giants, the "Quietest" Rooter Hits the Nail Squarely on the Nut.

By GYM BAGLEY.

There has been such a bridge crush of letters in answer to the query regarding the quiet rooter who roasted Larry Doyle before he made the swipe which won Monday's game that the postal guys are putting up a holler.

voy the idea of a duality it would have been more proper and consistent to have no stated, in either brackets or in a foot note.

Take the lighter phase of expression, the joke, with which if I may be pardoned for obtruding my own personality

McGraw had put his bunch on the car pet in the dressing room before the game, they meant it. It's too bad we couldn't have copped a snap shot of Jack Taylor's mug when those seven runs came over.

CAMERA NUT CAUSES ERUPTION AT TIMES

FIGHT BEE BUZZING AT SARATOGA TRACK

Since Leo Mayer Got Trimmed the Punching Craze Has Become Epidemic—Prominent Sports in a Clash.

By "TOMMY" TOMPKINS.

By Telegraph to The Evening Mail.

Saratoga, Aug. 22.—It's in the air. That's the surest thing you know. What? Why, the fight spirit. All hands here are on edge and are willing to go the limit at least provocation. Friends forget the association of years, and before they are aware of it are exchanging blows and trying to knock the block off each other.

First, it was a mixup between a newspaper man and Leo Mayer, a bookmaker. Mayer thought that he had the right to tell the reporter what to send into his paper, and as the latter objected, they came together. The newspaper man

"There is a man who owes me money and I am going to get it," he said.

He started for Walker and there was a brief exchange of compliments. These were followed by blows, and when it was all over it was hard to tell who had been hurt the most. At any rate there was an arrest, and Tom Woodford was the man who found himself in the custody of a village constable. He was charged with assault and at the preliminary hearing was held in $500 bail. Later there was a hearing at the police court and the bail was raised to $2,000, Woodford being held for the grand jury.

Brandt, who is the son of one of the most prominent attorneys in Chicago, declared after the court proceedings that he was the aggrieved party and that when

LUNATICS I HAVE MET—BY GOLDBERG.

HE ALWAY TAKES A SHOW VERY SERIOUSLY.

LOON VII

THE SHOW FIEND.

BAGLEY HAS A WEEP AS THE RAIN FALLS

But the Sun May Shine Again, Perhaps, and Then the Giants Will Increase Their Percentage at the Expense of St. Louis.

By GYM BAGLEY.

It is raining on the Polo Grounds and in consequence there is no game.

It is raining in other places, too, which fact, perhaps, sops up the spread of endeavor, but the Elsewhere is unimportant compared with the Here. The roar of events on the Polo Grounds is drowned. Nothing human lives between the plain of heretofore action and the low lying gloom of the crowding clouds. So may the Coliseum have looked when old Rome was no more. So may Broadway look when the Mad Peters has his way and Forty-second street is sunk to its reward in the sub-cellar of the final cremation.

And still it rains.

And there is no play, with Chicago only one measly game away.

Under the sheltering lee of the club house porch stands Harry Tuthill, in the fatigue undress of his trainer's calling, a flannel shirt and pants—not trousers. Harry only wears trousers to church—the one lone figure in the sodden silence of human sounds. A drop of Heaven's distilled water, glistening like a pearl in a setting of oak, hangs pendent from the Southern exposure of his wooden nose.

And the cataract continues to come down. I never knew one to come up.

From out the cold and clammy East the swirling wind tears holes in the curtain of rain. It slaps up against the stands and, angry at the resistance to its sway, comes back with spiteful spits that changes Tuthill's haven to the weather gauge and forces that seasoned chunk of athletic mold to duck behind the window panes.

There he loses the pearl.

But he can gaze out at the desolation the rain has wrought and say bad words because his pets are not humping their percentage at the expense of St. Louis, the while, perchance, Chicago is crawling up.

And more rain.

The elevated trains roll up to the station, but there is nothing sassy in their rattle. Their insides are as empty as the Recipient of Charity. George Gould is joining Tuthill in expressions not found in the Fourth Reader. The road of yesterday has been crabbed by another kind of water to-day.

And still the soggy hand of April, lingering after death, wipes out the smiles of May and keeps on squeezing the sponge.

To the Northeast, where the Harlem's tide is entertaining its sister waters from above and is swelled with pride thereat, the tall spire of a schooner's topmast points weeping to the sky for the ground that may be lost, with Chi-

GOLDBERG'S ESSAY ON THEATRICAL BUGS

BY R. L. GOLDBERG.

DETROIT USES YANKEE PLAY TO DEFEAT GRIFFITH'S TRIBE

By ALEXANDER MACKENZIE.

By Telegraph to The Evening Mail.

Detroit Mich., May 17.—Joe Doyle has been roasted so much since he broke into the big league about his slowness that he finally decided to hurry up in a game. He did it yesterday, but at the wrong time, and the Tigers have another notch in their sticks to denote a victory over the Yanks.

It was all right about the hastening stunt while Joe was pitching and he was getting away with it in good style, but when "Dutch" Schaefer bunted in the seventh inning with two out, and Cobb

STANDING OF THE CLUBS.

NATIONAL LEAGUE.						AMERICAN LEAGUE.					
Clubs.	W.	L.	PC.	Clubs.	W. L. PC.	Clubs.	W.	L.	PC.	Clubs.	W. L. PC.
New York..	21	3	.875	Boston ...	10 14 .417	Chicago ..	18	8	.692	Phila. ...	12 11 .522
Chicago ...	21	4	.840	Cincinnati..	8 15 .348	Detroit ...	14	9	.609	Boston ...	9 14 .391
Pittsburg	11	8	.579	St. Louis ...	6 19 .240	Cleveland	15	11	.577	Wash'n ...	7 16 .333
Phila. ...	13	10	.565	Brooklyn ..	5 19 .190	New York..	12	11	.522	St. Louis ...	8 17 .229

RESULTS OF YESTERDAY'S GAMES.

Chicago, 7; Boston, 0.
Pittsburg at Brooklyn.
Chicago at Boston.
Cincinnati at Philadelphia.
New York-St. Louis, Brooklyn-Pittsburg and Philadelphia-Cincinnati games postponed—rain.

Detroit, 3; New York, 0.
Cleveland, 2; Boston, 1.
Chicago, 7; Washington, 2.
St. Louis, 4; Philadelphia, 0.

GAMES SCHEDULED FOR TO-DAY.

St. Louis at New York—two games.
Pittsburg at Brooklyn.
Chicago at Boston.

New York at Detroit.
Philadelphia at St. Louis.
Boston at Cleveland.
Washington at Chicago.

"THE WHITE MAN'S BURDEN; OR, WHY JOHN WENT DIPP

KED AND CONTRACTS
TO NEW YORK GIANTS

**the Local Club—Season Will Open on April 16 — Cubs' Owner
w's Team Is to Be Feared Next Year.**

By J. J. KARPE.

er is being treated justly." But all
remains to be seen.
e plans for the trip to Marlin

in April comes on the ninth and this is
too early for an opening, the opening had
to be shoved back one week. It will

LUNATICS I HAVE MET---BY GOLDBERG.

LOON XVII

THE HOT-AIR MERCHANT.

EMPIRE TRACK IS SITUATED IN A PICTURESQUE COUNTRY

New Course Is Bounded by Beautifully Wooded and Hilly Land and Will Be as Easy of Access as Any Racing Plant in the Metropolitan Circuit.

By J. J. KARPF.

Now that it is definitely settled that there will be a race meeting at the Empire City track August 10 to 30, inclusive, this is a good time to let the racing patrons know what the course looks like.

There are thousands of patrons of the sport who never have been within miles of the Empire track, and it is this element that is belittling the plant, taking their cue from what they have heard uttered by a solitary few of those who are actively and financially interested in racing, and naturally are prejudiced.

The race course, which is located between Mount Vernon and Yonkers, near Mount Vernon and Yonkers when within sight of the course. The main entrance, which will be used mostly for automobiles at the coming meeting, is much on the order of Sheepshead Bay. Nine passes through lawns that are shaded and plentifully sprinkled with flower beds. All this meets the eye, and it is pleasing, too, as you approach the grand stand. At the entrance the first thing that you admire is a life-size stallion in bronze, something that was imported from France when the track was first built.

To the right are spots just suited for cooling out horses after a race. Beyond this is the paddock, back of one of the other side of the track, where the stand patrons would get more shade, and new steel and stone stands will be erected to accommodate the masses who are expected to patronize the track. The entire course is inclosed in a frame of densely wooded and hilly country.

The meeting this year will not see everything in perfect shape. It won't be impossible to do this, because there is much renovating to be done, the track having been sadly neglected. But the patrons will be able to make themselves comfortable this year. The betting ring is not very large, and if fifty bookmakers weigh in and the crowd is large...

YANKEES HUMBLED THE CHI. CHAMPEENS

White Sox Wilted When Griffith's Bunch Straightened Out the Slants of the Famous Nick Altrock—Their Rally Came Too Late.

STANDING OF THE CLUBS.

AMERICAN LEAGUE				NATIONAL LEAGUE			
Club	W.	L.	P.C.	Club	W.	L.	P.C.
Detroit	54	35	.607	Chicago	60	24	.714
Chicago	57	37	.606	Pittsburg	56	34	.622
Phila	53	38	.580	New York	54	39	.600
Cleveland	54	39	.581	Washington	29	60	.315

Boston	41	47	.478	Cincinnati	39	53	.423
New York	37	53	.411	Brooklyn	41	53	.436
St. Louis	30	55	.398	Boston	38	52	.422
Washn	28	60	.318	St. Louis	22	76	.224

RESULTS OF YESTERDAY'S GAMES.

New York, 7, Chicago, 5.
Detroit, 3, Washington, 2. First game.
Detroit, 9, Washington, 4. Second game.
Boston, 10, St. Louis, 3.
Philadelphia, 8, Cleveland, 1.

Chicago, 6, New York, 0.
Pittsburg, 6, Brooklyn, 3.
Cincinnati, 5, Boston, 2.
Philadelphia, 5, St. Louis, 1.

GAMES SCHEDULED FOR TO-DAY.

Chicago at New York.
Detroit at Washington.
St. Louis at Boston.
Cleveland at Philadelphia.

New York at Chicago.
Brooklyn at Pittsburg.
Boston at Cincinnati.
Philadelphia at St. Louis.

By GYM BAGLEY.

BALLOONATICS I HAVE MET---BY GOLDBERG.

BAGLEY PRODS BINGHAM.

Explains New Sport Dish and Tells How Cop's Time Is Wasted Hunting Harmless Referees and Boxers.

By GYM BAGLEY.

Dear Bagley—In yesterday's Evening Mail you ask me if I had used "Bingham's Sport Crabettes." I must confess I haven't. But I will if you will inform me what "Bingham's Sport Crabettes" are and where I may obtain them.

Yours very kindly,
BO

Kidding your old pal, eh? And after all I've said to you. You've never taken any of Bingham's Sport Crabettes, never? Why, you boob, you're stuffed with them. Every time you walk abroad you rattle with the B. S. C. When you are aroused in the subway they stick out all over you like the redistilled spots of a too enthusiastic jag. You're a perfectly pathetic ad for them.

But it isn't your fault. You happen to live in New York and can't help it. You're a victim of the force of example. And I'm with you. I'm in the boob class, too. We all are.

Once upon a time there was a Captain of Industry who wanted it All. He was a greedy gee and wouldn't split with the herd who were doing the Work. He didn't even want to split 90 and 10. But this particular herd were a Tough Bunch and it was in a Lonely Country where a solid punch in the jaw might back up the Constitution and have no respect for a Supreme Court decision regarding the privileges of Vested Rights.

The Captain had a foreman who was Wise to the Situation and made a spiel...

that guy and He'll take care of the bunch."

And that's it, Bo. You fall for the Big Badge.

Commissioner Bingham has admitted that he was unable to cope with the wave of crime in this city. Of course he didn't have to commit himself, everybody knew that. But he had an excuse. Incompetency always has some Prince Albert an excuse. He didn't have policemen enough.

A few weeks ago there was an arrest at Bull's Elmore's Consolidated Athletic club. It took Eleven Policemen to make the arrest. Three men were pinched, two boxers and a referee. These three were Desperate Men. They had a long Record of Crime before them and the Police Force could take no chances. A postal card addressed to these culprits would have insured their presence at a station house, but, of course, that isn't according to the police ritual—except with burglars.

The Eleven spent five or six hours that evening gathering in the two boxers and the ref. The next morning in court the Eleven were on the job from 9 o'clock to the afternoon.

And their time was Wasted. The court laughed at the charge. The three desperadoes were released. And the ref—some one you know well, too, Bo—and a goodly proportion of the Eleven had a quart of ice cream soda and soaked up to the Next Time It happened.

IS BALLOONING A MANIA?

Goldberg Says the Latest Sport Is O.-K. for Those Who Are Tired...

CAMP AND HINKEY TO GET BUSY SOON

New Haven, Conn., Oct. 23.—Walter Camp was at the football practice yesterday. He watched the men very closely, especially when the forward passes were tried. When Hinkey arrives, there will be a conference of coaches to discuss the team and invent new plays.

This has been done every fall, and the result of last year's meeting was the tremendous improvement which won Yale the championship. Another result was...

KICK ON FOOTBALL RULES

Experts Say It Is Unfair to Allow Four Points on Field Goal—Gives Small Teams Advantage.

By ALEXANDER MACKENZIE.

The success of the new rules in this year's football games has set most of the critics thinking of further changes, and the result is an agitation to have the rules amended so that goals made from place or drop kicks will not have the same value that is now attached to their accomplishment.

The drop kick is one of the strong points of the small colleges and several of them have made it uncomfortable for the big fellows in the early season games. The victory by Penn State over the Cornell team by two field goals, while the Ithacans were making one touchdown, has started the talk of amendment afresh until there is now so much agitation that it seems that the rules committee will have to take notice and offer some change in the scoring rules at its next meeting.

Four points are now allowed for a goal from placement or from a drop kick, whereas a touchdown counts five points. The opponents of the kicking game claim that the reward for hard work in making a touchdown should be far greater than that for kicking a goal from thirty or forty yards from the line. It is easy for...

there are more drop kickers on the minor teams than can be overcome by the heavy work of the big colleges.

The large colleges do not think it dignified to try drop kicks against their weaker rivals, and therefore try to score by straight football, with the result that while they are laboriously working the ball the entire length of the field to make five points, the other team has made a couple of kicks and gains more points than can be overcome by one touchdown. It is this point that is causing the comment. The coaches and players of the teams which have no kickers are anxious to have the scoring system changed so that two goals from the field will equal one touchdown.

The coaches and players of the small colleges or the large ones, who are fortunate enough to have a good kicker, think that four points are not too much and will oppose any change, arguing that the skill necessary to kick a goal should be properly rewarded, and that if the other colleges cannot develop a man good enough to win points for his team in that manner, they should not try to put the college out of business who have taken the pains to turn out drop kickers.

Both sides have a little room for argu-

LUNATICS I HAVE MET---BY GOLDBERG

BAGLEY TELLS "WHO STRUCK PATTERSON"

By GYM BAGLEY.

GOLDBERG DISCOVERS NEW MANIA

By R. L. GOLDBERG.

"Why so sad, old man?"
"I have met with a terrible misfortune."
"Speak up. Maybe I can help you."
"No, kind sir, I'm ruined for life. This afternoon I ran over a man without killing him instantly. Woe is me!"

YANKS' REAL STRENGTH WILL BE KNOWN SOON

6

LUNATICS I HAVE MET—BY GOLDBERG.

ON THE STREET.

HE USUALLY GETS IN HIS HEAVIEST LICKS BEFORE POUNDING THE HAY.

HE ALWAYS MAKES HIMSELF BELIEVE THAT IT IS DOING HIM A WORLD OF GOOD

EVEN DURING WORKING HOURS.

LOON VIII

THE PHYSICAL CULTURE MANIAC.

MIKE AND HIS PAL ON WATER WAGON

Return After Being Lost Since Last Thursday and Hit Up the Sarsaparilla and Milk and Carbonic.

By GYM BAGLEY.

Well, they have discovered MIKE and his pal, THE SCHOLAR. These cronies pegged it home from Philadelphia, arriving late last night in time to hear the good news from Cincinnati, where the Cincinnati Reds put the screws on the Cubs, and, when the pair who have been tied in a sailor knot with the Cubs for first place, MIKE wanted to put in a load of fuel, but THE SCHOLAR reneged.

THE SCHOLAR—Pithy, Me illiterate chum, you will be exterminating your inner workings if you heave in any more fuel, so it is back to the Aqua for you my dearie. As for myself, I shall not taste of the vile fluid again, not—well, not until those people with the paste physiognomies from the city that borders on the Lake de Boreas come back to New York and beat the Giants two

team swallow? Incidentally Chance takes a fling at Bresnahan for wearing shin guards, and says Bres is not game, because he is afraid of being spiked.

I can't see where a man's gameness should be questioned simply because he is taking a precaution against being spiked to ribbons. If a man coming home late at night had an inkling that he might be sandbagged he would wear a skull protector. Chance might just as well say that a catcher or an umpire is not game because he wears a mask and does not take a chance of having his face dented by a foul tip.

Chance and Murphy called on Harry Pulliam before they started west and asked to have Bresnahan suspended and fined for inciting a riot. But they received a cold reception, because Mr. Pulliam was at the game in question and saw everything that took place.

PA TEN EYCK VS. SON TEN EYCK

Madison, Wis., May 27.—Next Friday, for the first time in boating history, an eastern university crew will race with a western university in western waters, when the crews of Syracuse university will measure strength and skill against the crews of the University of Wisconsin on the waters of Lake Mendota.

It is to be Ten Eyck against Ten Eyck father. Ten Eyck the elder is coach of the Syracuse crews, his son the coach of the Wisconsin crews, and the rivalry between father and son adds not a little to the interest which is taken in the race.

PHYSICAL CULTURE GERM PREVALENT

Once It Gets Into Your System It Takes a Full Nelson Hold and Then It Sticks Like Cement.

By R. L. GOLDBERG.

Did you ever walk into your old man's bedroom just as he was about to retire and discover him hanging to the gas jet by the lapel of his ear? Or, did you ever find the guy who works next to you at the office trying to hold his breath for half an hour and waving his arms in the air like a Dutch windmill? If you have ever encountered either of these during your rambles through life, then you need no introduction to the physical culture lunatic.

The magazine advs. advancing arguments in favor of physical exercise, at so much per argument, have won over so many supporters to the cause of muscular development that they could combine themselves into a national party and run a candidate for President. A picture of an arm with muscles on it like watermelons will inspire the ambitiously inclined to fall for a correspondence course in the Bududor system, or whatever name the owner of the arm chooses to call his muscular secret.

The nut will go through enough contortions every evening to make his liver do a flip and land somewhere up near his windpipe. After his course of about six months is finished and he is good and ripe for the junk dealer, he will look at his emaciated features in the mirror and exclaim:

LUNATICS I HAVE MET---BY GOLDBERG.

HIS STUFF SOUNDS LIKE A SERIES OF EXPLOSIONS FROM THE GAS ENGINE OF AN AUTOMOBILE

EVERY COLLEGE EVENT IS AN OCCASION FOR ONE OF THOSE LOVING, CONFIDENTIAL, PATRIOTIC, BROTHERLY SOUSES.

OWOO!

REMINDED THE OLD GEEK OF THE DAYS WHEN HE WAS A ROOTER AT COLLEGE.

LOON XXXV
THE COLLEGE ROOTER

HE CAN PUT A CAPE ON THE BUM QUICKER THAN AN EARTHQUAKE.

NO CHANGE IN RACE FOR PENNANT.

Athletics Count Upon Double-Header at Washington to Tie Things Up Again.

Hughey Dougherty, Philadelphia's champion rooter, and his companions in bugdom are happier over the fact that the Athletics have succeeded in breaking up an old tradition than they have been over anything Mack's outfit has done in some time.

The White Elephants had lost the first game of seven out of nine series up to yesterday, and Dougherty feared the hoodoo more than he did the Naps. Now, however, that the unlucky first set-to has been safely taken care of, the Philadelphia fans are offering all kinds of odds that two more will follow the same way.

They see another little ray of sunshine

have won only two. Jennings and his bunch are more than confident of breaking that losing streak, but——

There never was a team that was so enthusiastic over its chances as the Tigers. The strain under which they have been playing during the last three or four weeks is commencing to show. Not on the field, mind you, but after the game.

astic than the members of his team. He firmly believes he has the best team in either league and cannot see any way in which he can be beaten out.

Yesterday again they gave an exhibition of the spirit that has won more games for them this year than anything else—that of fighting an uphill battle

BASEBALL SITUATION AT A GLANCE.

The following table shows just what a defeat or a victory to-day will mean to the two leading clubs in the race for the American league pennant:

	WIN TWO.			LOSE TWO.			BREAK EVEN.		
Detroit	91	56	.619	89	58	.605	90	57	.612
	WIN.			LOSE.					
Philadelphia.	85	55	.607	84	56	.600			

NOISE LOON IS WITH US

Academic Youth Who Gives Vent to His Feelings in Eskimo and Turkish Lingo Has the Floor.

By R. L. GOLDBERG.

Bring in the strait jacket, we've got to his vest, the horrible truth was—

THE LID ON TIGHT AGAIN

Bingham's Disturbers Visited the Consolidated Club and Used the Hook, and Things Look Dubious for the "Order of Fistic Stars."

By GYM BAGLEY.

It's just as I predicted, Bo. The fight game is crabbed again. Maybe the smoke will blow away after a bit and there will be some more local boxing, but just at present we will have to ride to Philadelphia or see no fights at all.

Up at the Consolidated A. C. they have been conducting things legitimately and there was every reason to believe that the show scheduled for last night would come off as per schedule. But there was nothing "making," because a policeman with a gold badge paved with emeralds told Boss Elmer that orders from Mulberry street "made it imperative for him to stop the entertainment." The officials of the club do not take kindly to riding in a patrol wagon, so the 300 members present were offered their choice between a lecture on club rights or dismissal. They hiked for the elevators and got out into the bright rays of Lincoln square.

There is no telling how long the lid is going to be kept screwed down. This

supposed to have been uttered by Joe Gans. The dinge is credited with handing the lightweight championship to Memsic—whatever that means. Gans says he has retired from the ring, and as he considers Memsic the best lightweight outside of himself, he hands the honors, with great pleasure, to the Chicago boy. It's a joke. What right has Gans to present any championships? These titles are fought for, not handed out as promiscuously as cigarette coupons. But, then, I guess some of the other lightweights who have it on Memsic will not lose any sleep because of Gans's generosity. And people must not take that bout of the other night seriously. Gans could have put Memsic away in a few rounds. He let him stay the limit because there was a bit of tainted money to be had. Gans simply can't remain on the level.

We hear that Bill Squires is coming East looking for work. The more the

LUNATICS THAT I HAVE MET--BY GOLDBERG.

LOON II
THE FIGHT BUG.

TERRIBLE TAPIOCA, WHO GUARANTEES TO PUT JEFF AWAY IN ONE ROUND.

HE WILL ALWAYS FALL FOR THE NEW HEAVYWEIGHT LEMONE.

HE CAN SIT IN THE VILEST ATMOSPHERE AND STILL BREATHE.

GOLDBERG DISCOVERS NEW BRAND

By R. L. GOLDBERG.

After putting the maniac in a strait-jacket and loading his system with a ton of hop, the commission of eminent alienists, headed by old Doc Bull, was able to get a line on the fight bug's long suit in the dementia department. The loon experts doped out the following report on the sanity—or, rather, the insanity—of the scrapus nutus:

"We find that the subject's brain is a trifle dusty in places, and consequently the wheels therein located are somewhat retarded in their rotary action. In consequence, said nut is sluggish in perceiving that he is the goat. In other words, or the same words (whichever way you like best), he will fall for anything in the fistic line that is shoved in his direction. He has an abnormal capacity for being stung. He is just as willing to cough up ten dollars as ten cents to see a couple of feeble-minded cheese peddlers get together in a hand-me-down ring and negotiate a slugfest that would do a pair of crippled nanny goats proud. All he needs is a little press-agent junk, a shifty performer at his side whispering low-down into his ear, and he is good for a month's salary.

"He realizes in a measure that he is being fed to bunk stuff, but invariably

BAGLEY DISHES UP SOME EXPERT TESTIMONY FOR MAIL READERS

Enlightens the Baseball Fan as Regards Willie Keeler's Past—Other

By GYM BAGLEY.

very loudly: "Now, kid, get after him; knock the kike's head off." And to think of it, this is the very man now that or-

As Regards Chase's Salary, You Must Ask the Man Who Is

COLD WEATHER PLAYS
HAVOC WITH PITCHERS

SUPERBAS REQUIRE GINGER

FIGHTERS WALK THROUGH THE STREETS IN THEIR FIGHTING TOGS.

A MAN STR FOR CONEY ISLAND IN BATHING SU

KIMONOS FOR BALL PLAYERS

EVENING DRESS A LA TWAIN

THERE IS STILL A LOT OF FIGHT IN THE GIANTS

With the Odds Against Them the Team Pulls Together and Overcomes Great Obstacles—McGrawites' Chances Coming.

That twelfth-inning finish on Saturday did remind one of the old team of

short trips to Philadelphia and Brooklyn will follow. These two trips are the

GOOD FIGHT BILLED FOR THIS WEEK

Tommy Murphy and Rouse O'Brien have gone into training for their coming bout at the Sharkey A. C. on Friday evening.

Murphy is at Stradford, Conn., in charge of Kid Broad, who is assisted by Amby McGarry, Young Otto and a number of other good boys, while O'Brien is

TTIRE CRAZE----BY GOLDBERG.

THAT PIKER SMITH IS PALMING OFF AN OLD QUILT FOR A BATH-ROBE

AND HE ONLY TOLD ME LAST NIGHT THAT HE HAD SO MUCH MONEY IT HURT HIM

FOR THEY CALL ME A BATH-ROBE GIRL

BATH-ROBES THE REAL PIZZAZ ON BROADWAY

- SOCIAL JOTTINGS -

WE TAKE PLEASURE IN ANNOUNCING THAT AUGUSTUS Q. FISHCAKE, THE MILLIONAIRE BUTTON-HOLE MAKER, TOOK A BATH LAST WEDNESDAY - HE WAS FLOODED WITH CONGRATULATIONS FROM HIS MANY FRIENDS.

SOCIETY FOLK WILL FOLLOW MARK'S EXAMPLE AND INFORM THE WORLD EVERY TIME THEY TAKE A BATH

FORMER YANKS USUALLY TRIM GRIFFITH'S TEAM

Somehow the Ex-New Yorkers Put on Steam When They Leave This Burg and Rub It in on Their Former Teammates.

IT IS NOT A CRIME TO REVIVE A GOOD THING

Bagley Sets Right a Doubting Thomas and Tells Him About That Sullivan-Kilrain Affair Eighteen Years Ago.

By GYM BAGLEY.

Dear Bagley—Can you tell me when John L. Sullivan and Jake Kilrain fought and something of that memorable battle? I have had an argument with a friend of mine about the date and place. I contend that it was in 1900, the year the Horton law went out of kelter, and that they fought at New Orleans.

You can set me right if you will.

THOMAS MANNING.

My dear Thomas, you are away off; nowheres near it at all. The Horton law had nothing to do with the Sullivan-Kilrain affair; it wasn't that kind of a festival.

They fought at Richburg Mills, a hamlet about ninety miles from New Orleans, July 8, 1889, for the championship of the world. It was on the turf, bare knuckles, and London rules governed. Sullivan won in the seventy-fifth round.

It was one of the most important battles in the history of the ring. All kinds of guys were interested in it. The licensed vender on Avenue A got there

Mike Donovan called for Pat Kendricks, of New Orleans. The Sullivan corner objected. Jimmy Wakely jumped into the ring and named John Fitzpatrick, also of New Orleans. Donovan insisted and Mitchell proposed they toss a coin. Muldoon put up a kick against this and finally Mitchell agreed to accept Fitzpatrick.

The referee then made a little spiel in which he said that he wasn't thoroughly familiar with the rules, but that he would do the best he could.

Charley Johnson handed Sullivan $1,000 to bet on himself, which amount was immediately covered by Kilrain and the money placed in the referee's hands.

Sullivan was never in better condition, before or since. Kilrain seemed to lack the springiness of step and jauntiness of air that marked the champion. But this might have been due to caution. And indeed Jake began the fight very carefully.

Sullivan took an early lead and in the fifth round had Kilrain worried with smashes to the stomach. This caused

To the Ladies, Bless Them

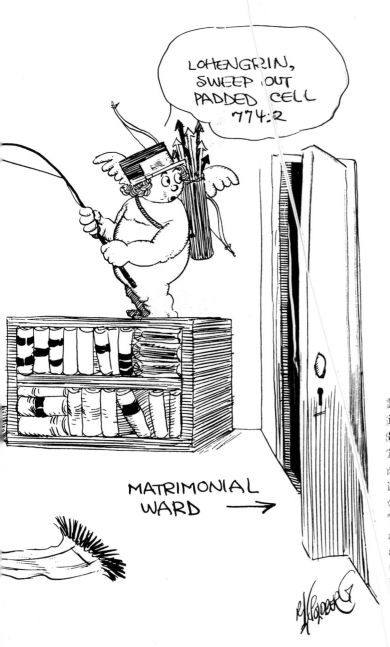

I would say my most successful cartoons were some in *The Evening Mail* that helped me impress Irma Seeman with my future. Then this one appeared in *The Evening Mail,* her picture inset, when we were married Oct. 17, 1916. Another part of the strip is reproduced overleaf, with a recent picture of Irma with me. A family picture would include our sons, Thomas Reuben and George Warren, their wives and our grandchildren. Thomas is an artist, whose abstracts are in museums and private collections. George is a theatrical and motion picture producer internationally, with headquarters now in London.

● In his response to the tributes paid him at the luncheon staged in 1963 by the National Cartoonists Society, the Guest of Honor said, "Success is 40 percent luck, 20 percent talent and in my own case the other forty percent's Irma" —a reference to the lady who sat with him on the dais.

I USE DR. BONEYARD'S PHONOGRAPH RECORDS FOR MY REDUCING EXERCISES BECAUSE THEY'RE MORE EXPENSIVE THAN THE OTHERS- AND I STICK TO MY DIET VERY CLOSELY _ I NEVER EAT MORE THAN SIX EGGS FOR BREAKFAST AND MAKE IT A STRICT RULE NEVER TO EAT ANY LUNCH - OF COURSE, I MAY EAT SEVEN OR EIGHT PORTIONS OF ICE CREAM AND A DOZEN PIECES OF CAKE AT AN AFTERNOON MAH JONGG PARTY, BUT I NEVER LET THAT INTERFERE WITH MY APPETITE FOR DINNER - HAVE YOU HEARD WHAT THEY ARE DOING IN PARIS TO REDUCE? THE FASHIONABLE WOMEN ARE ALL RUBBING THEMSELVES WITH A MIXTURE OF PRUNE-JUICE AND FOUNTAIN-PEN INK - I HEARD - ETC. ETC.

THE BABY ELEPHANT WHO IS CONTINUALLY "REDUCING" AND WEIGHS MORE THAN EVER.

THIS WEATHER IS JUST RIGHT FOR A FINE WALK AND A NICE LITTLE TALK

ISN'T THAT HAT SIMPLY STUNNING!

I HAD A FINE DAY AT THE OFFICE, DEAR- I SOLD 66 ORDERS OF DOLL GLUE

THAT DRESS WOULD LOOK LOVELY WITH MY RED SHOES

ANABELLE PHYLLIS CHRYSANTHEMUM PAGE WAS A RAVISHING BEAUTY WHEN SEEN ON THE STAGE,

WHILE LILLIAN GREEN NEVER BROKE ANY HEARTS, FOR SHE ALWAYS APPEARED IN THE COMICAL PARTS;

BUT LIFE IS PECULIAR WHEREVER WE ROAM, HERE'S A PICTURE OF ANNABELLE PHYLLIS AT HOME,

WHILE, WITHOUT HER DISGUISE, HERE IS LILLIAN GREEN, SHE'S A PEACH AND A BEAUTY- IN FACT, SHE'S A QUEEN!

107

109

PUBLIC ENEMY NO. 27

THE MAN WHO INVENTED SCALES.

WHILE MRS. SOBB IS CALLED TO THE TELEPHONE DURING A MEETING IN HER HOUSE, ALL THE OTHER MEMBERS SNEAK OUT INTO THE KITCHEN AND TRY TO STEAL THE MAID SHE HAS HAD FOR EIGHT YEARS.

112

6

All A Lotta Boloney

It is well known, of course, that nations have their individual tastes in humor. One form which appeals especially to Americans is to invent jazzy-sounding substitutes for much-used words. We have it on good authority that money and drink have many score verbal variations. But America's pet word, although its alternatives are not nearly so numerous, is that which relates to attempted deception on the part of our fellow men. Our native inclination is to hate artificiality, affectation or pretense. The various degrees of this we refer to with such expressions as bunk, bluff, fake, hokum, hooey, con, apple sauce, banana oil, putting on the dog, high-hatting, ritzing, and so on.

We hear a candidate for public office say, "If I'm elected I'll give this city the first honest administration it has had in thirty-two years," and we sensibly conclude that he's "filling us with a lot of hot air." We do a great deal of expressing ourselves in terms of slang, and it seems to please our imagination most when we can devise some odd-sounding word or phrase that applies to the ancient art of sham. Notice

how quickly the public pounces on any such expression produced by a comic artist or humorist. A great deal of slang now in current use has been manufactured in this way.

Once I was in Cleveland attending the World Series between the Indians and the then Brooklyn Dodgers. Morris Gest was presenting *Aphrodite,* a spectacle play, at one of the local theaters. He invited the visiting newspapermen to attend. With several friends I dropped in when the show was about half over and stood up in the rear of the theater taking in the elaborate stage effects. A Philadelphia man, an ardent follower of baseball, whose name I have forgotten, was a member of our party. This chap was usually around with the newspapermen and was known as quite a character. His line of slang was classical; if he had happened to have selected comic art as a profession he would have given the world many expressions which have never become well known, because he was without the medium to popularize them.

When the big scene of the play came, embellished with all the flourish Morris Gest al-

THADDEUS T. VEAL SAYS: "THE PEOPLE HAVE SPOKEN— NOW THEY CAN BE DEAF AND DUMB FOR FOUR YEARS MORE."

STANLEY J. CHILLBLAINS SAYS: "THINGS TURNED OUT JUST AS I PREDICTED— I SAID THAT, NO MATTER WHO WAS ELECTED, A LARGE NUMBER OF AMERICANS WOULD STILL CONTINUE TO CHOKE ON FISH BONES."

WARWICK T. GLUM SAYS: "THE RESULT OF THE ELECTION SUITS ME—I'M NOT A PARTY MAN— I DO BUSINESS WITH ALL PARTIES— I'M AN UNDERTAKER."

ways gave his shows, most of the audience sat enraptured with the magnificence of the display. Apparently everybody in the theater but one was deeply moved. The business man from Philadelphia was the single exception. With a wave of disgust, he walked toward the entrance, remarking as he started to leave, "That's just a lot of boloney."

Such a descriptive phrase for such an event! Contrasting so sharply with the solemnity of the moment, it struck me as one of the funniest lines I had ever heard. And subconsciously I must have recorded it in my mind, for after the first good laugh I never thought about it again until six years later, when I was sitting at my easel board one day trying to dope out a live filler.

Then I got to thinking generally about the word "boloney." Boloney sausage is a funny sort of thing anyway, and in the sense that most people like it and hate to admit they do, it is similar to sauerkraut and corned beef and cabbage. Why had it never been used to any extent in cartooning? The only explanation I could find was that the word didn't mean a thing when spelled correctly — Bologna. Everybody under the sun called it boloney — a marvelous moniker in itself — and nobody would know what you were talking about if you pronounced it the right way.

HERSHALL PIPP
SAYS :

" I CONGRATULATE
THE DEFEATED
CANDIDATES -
THEY WILL NOT
BE PUT TO
THE TROUBLE
OF BREAKING
THEIR ELECTION
PROMISES. "

FERDINAND R. STATIC
SAYS : " I AM TICKLED
TO DEATH - THE SPEECHES
ARE OVER AND NOW I
CAN GET SOME MUSIC
ON MY RADIO. "

RUBE GOLDBERG

I TOLD YOU SO!

YES YOU DID - BOLONEY!

115

A WEALTHY MAN NAMED SIMPSON TOOK A JOURNEY TO A LAND, WHERE THE WEATHER WAS REPUTED TO BE ELEGANT AND GRAND,

WHILE A POOR, DEJECTED TRAVELING MAN, NAMED AARON J. O'LEARY HAD TO TRAVEL TO A CITY THAT WAS DISMAL, DAMP AND DREARY:

BUT SIMPSON HAD AN AWFUL TIME AND SUFFERED MENTAL PAIN, FOR HE RAN INTO A SEASON FULL OF RAIN, RAIN, RAIN,

WHILE THE WEATHER WHERE O'LEARY WENT WAS BEAUTIFUL AND SWELL, WHICH JUST ILLUSTRATES HOW TRUTHFUL IS THE SAYING, "WHO CAN TELL?"

THE WEATHER HERE IS PERFECT ALL THE TIME

BOLONEY!

BUGHOUSE

LISTEN, NAPOLEON — THERE MUST BE SOME MISTAKE — I DON'T WANT TO COMPLAIN, BUT THOSE GUYS LOOK MUCH NUTTIER THAN US

THERE'S NO DOUBT OF IT, JULIUS CAESAR — WE'RE LUCKY TO BE IN HERE WHERE THEY CAN'T HURT US

LET'S CLOSE UP THE COUNTRY — THE WORLD'S SERIES IS ON

I KNOW WHAT EVERY PLAYER ON BOTH TEAMS HAD FOR BREAKFAST

YOW!

I THINK I CAN GET HOLD OF TWO TICKETS FOR $66, APIECE

I BET ALL MY WIFE'S JEWELS ON WASHINGTON

I BET MY CHILDREN'S UNDERWEAR ON PITTSBURGH

YOU DESERVE SYMPATHY FOR BEING LESS FORTUNATE THAN PEOPLE ON THE OUTSIDE

NUT FACTORY

BOLONEY — A LOT OF PEOPLE ON THE OUTSIDE OUGHT TO BE IN HERE, TOO!

It was in this manner the filler, *"That's a lot of boloney,"* came into my cartoons. That it caught on well is undoubtedly due to the fact that it furnishes another means to indulge our favorite hobby of branding anything a fake. As good as the word "boloney" is itself and as much as this mysterious food product appeals to our vein of humor, I doubt whether it would ever have gone over if it had not been for the supplementary factor that Americans are keen for any new way to describe hoodwinking.

WHEN "THUG" McSLUG WAS FINALLY ARRESTED AFTER KILLING 16 POLICEMEN AND WOUNDING 74 PASSERS-BY, HIS MOTHER SAID, "THUG IS ONLY A BIG, MISUNDERSTOOD, OVERGROWN BOY — IF HE KILLED THOSE POLICEMEN, I'M SURE IT WAS ALL DONE IN A SPIRIT OF FUN."

HORRIBLE HANK, THE SOUTH SIDE SNAKE, SET FIRE TO NINE HOSPITALS AND ROBBED 88 TRAINS— WHEN HE WAS CAUGHT, HIS SWEETHEART SAID, "THE PUBLIC DOES NOT UNDERSTAND MY HANK— HE HAS A HEART OF GOLD— HE BRINGS ME AN APPLE EVERY DAY— I WILL STICK TO HIM BECAUSE I AM THE ONLY ONE WHO KNOWS THAT HE IS A GENTLEMAN."

WHEN SAM THE SLASHER WAS FOUND CARVING UP THE REMAINS OF FIVE WOMEN HE HAD MURDERED, HIS DEVOTED SISTER SAID, "EVERY BOY MUST SOW HIS WILD OATS— IF HE IS LET ALONE I'M SURE HE WILL COME OUT ALL RIGHT"

WHISKERS, WHISKERS, NEW-MOWN HAY, HORSE'S WOULD RATHER EAT WHISKERS, WHISKERS, AND HIS WHISKERS GROODLE-OODLE-OO

WHEN PETE BLACKJACK WAS CONVICTED OF POISON-ING A WHOLE FAMILY OF TWELVE, HIS GRANDMOTHER SAID, "IT WAS ONLY A CHILDISH PRANK— PETE ISN'T REALLY GROWN UP— HE HAS THE SONG OF MIS-CHIEVOUS YOUTH IN HIS HEART— I CAN'T UNDERSTAND THE JURY"

YOUR HONOR, MY BOY ISN'T REALLY BAD. HE STEALS BECAUSE HE'S AN INNOCENT BABY AT HEART

BOLONEY- HE WEARS LONG PANTS AND MUST ACCEPT THE RESPONSIBILITIES THAT GO WITH THEM— 30 DAYS!

117

ALL TOO HUMAN

RUBE BEANSOUP COMES
TO CARVARD STRAIGHT FROM
THE FARM IN BUMVILLE

IN HIS SOPHOMORE YEAR HE
CULTIVATES THE PANCAKE
LID AND THE COFFIN NAIL

IN HIS JUNIOR YEAR HE BECOMES
THE HERO OF THE VARSITY ELEVEN,
HAS ALL THE SWELL DAMES AT
HIS FEET AND IS LOVINGLY
CALLED "RECKLESS RUBE,
    THE ROUGH-HOUSE ROUSTABOUT"
HIS NAME IS A BYWORD IN
    EVERY COLLEGE IN THE COUNT

ONCE UPON A TIME THERE
WAS A BOY NAMED THADDEUS
ZUMP WHO TOSSED SUCH
A NIFTY TODDLE THAT
ALL THE FLAPPERS KEPT
HIM JAZZING TWENTY
FOUR HOURS A DAY.

WHILE A POOR IRON-
HOOFED DUMBELL
NAMED BOZO McDUFF
WAS SO DEAD IN HIS
DOGS HE HAD TO STOP
GOING TO DANCES
BECAUSE ALL THE JANES
SHUNNED HIM LIKE SMALL POX.

BUT ZUMP DANCED HIS
YOUNG LIFE AWAY AND
LATER FOUND HIS BANK-
ROLL AS BARE AS A
CHORUS GIRL'S BACK. SO
HE TOOK A JOB AS NIGHT
WATCHMAN OUTSIDE THE
DANCE-HALL AND NEVER
SHOOK ANOTHER SHIMMY.

WHILE CLUMSY BOZO
McDUFF HAD SO MUCH
TIME TO WORK, HE
MADE OODLES OF JACK
AND, LATER IN LIFE, ALL
THE QUEENS FELT HONORED
WHEN HE DRAGGED
THEM AROUND THE ROOM
FOR A SHIN-BRUISING
FOOT-BATTLE - ALL THIS
DOESN'T RHYME, BUT THE
IDEA IS POETIC, ANYWAY!

COLLEGE."===*By Goldberg.*

AFTER GRADUATION HIS LIFE BF- IS A BLANK - NOBODY KNOWS OR CARES WHAT BECOMES OF HIM.

DURING HIS SENIOR YEAR, HE CULTIVATES THAT CLASSIC AIR OF STUDIED CARELESSNESS AND BECOMES SO TERRIBLY GREAT THAT IT HURTS HIM TO THINK

HE FINALLY LOOMS UP UNDER A CHIN MOP AS THE FOURTH-ASSISTANT BOOKEEPER IN A WHOLESALE SHIRT-WAIST HOUSE - SUCH IS FAME !

POLICE PATROL

LITTLE ROCOCO MANDAMUS McSNARK IN A BEAUTIFUL CARRIAGE WAS PUSHED THROUGH THE PARK,

WHILE A BABY NAMED MACY TOLEDO McFIGG RODE AROUND IN THIS SAD-LOOKING SORT OF A RIG :

BUT FATE MORE THAN EVER'S BEYOND OUR CONTROL, NOW McSNARK ONLY RIDES IN THE COPPERS' PATROL.

WHILE McFIGG HAS GROWN RICH, AS CAN PLAINLY BE SEEN, AND HE RIDES ALL AROUND IN THIS GRAND LIMOUSINE.

This letter-head sure has a prosperous look, it contains as much dope as a page from a book,

While the firm of Pizzaro, McGinnis and Draper, writes all correspondence on this simple paper:

But, look, gentle stranger—this picture portrays "The Wonder" on one of its busiest days,

While here we are happy to picture, in turn, the Pizzaro, McGinnis and Draper concern

Edward Milwaukee Seattle McSwerve, when speaking in public had plenty of nerve,

While fear almost killed Alexander McLeach, when he thought he'd be asked to deliver a speech:

But, at home, Eddie looked like a terrible sap, for he hadn't the courage to open his trap,

While Alex could talk himself blue in the face, when at home he made speeches all over the place!

124

If you examine the makeup of the word "Profiteer" you will find that it includes all of us.

SEEING HISTORY AT CLOSE RANGE

The Experiences of an American Cartoonist

While Marooned in France During the

Outbreak of the Present European War

BY

R. L. GOLDBERG

*The Evening Mail's
Inimitable Cartoonist*

Originator of

"Foolish Questions," "I'm the Guy,"
"Phoney Films," "What are You
Gonna Do With It," "I'm Cured," etc.

IF YOU ARE ON THE GROUND, NATURALLY YOU CAN UNDERSTAND THE WAR SITUATION MORE THOROUGHLY

THE ONLY TIME YOU DON'T NEED A PASSPORT IS WHEN YOU HAVE ONE

THE SAFEST PLACE IN EUROPE RIGHT NOW IS THE BATTLEFIELD

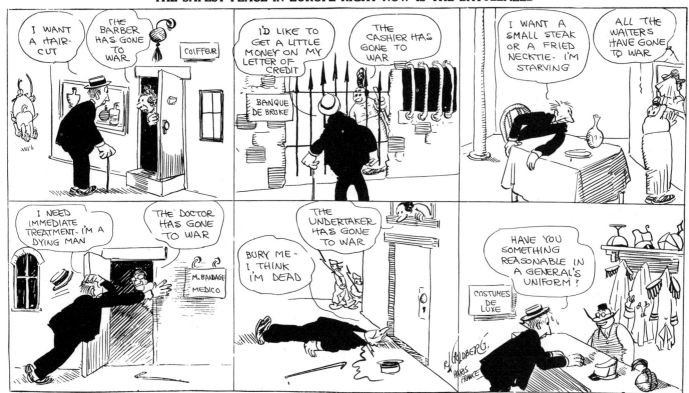

THE ONLY THING YOU CAN CALL YOUR OWN IN WARTIME IS YOUR INDIGNATION

WE'D LIKE TO WALK BACK, BUT ALL THE SHOE STORES IN PARIS ARE CLOSED

MOBILIZATION AND KISSING MEAN THE SAME THING IN PARIS

THE ONLY THING YOU CAN SMUGGLE IN FROM EUROPE NOW IS A HEADACHE

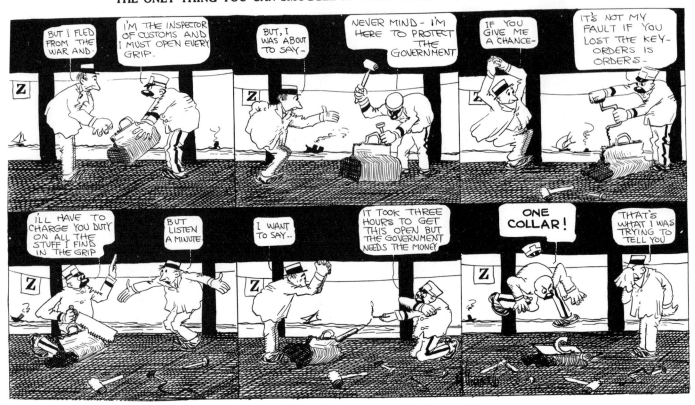

YOU'D THINK THE AMERICAN REFUGEES HAD SOMETHING TO DO WITH STARTING THE WAR

AND STILL WE'RE WONDERING WHY THE FOLKS AT HOME DON'T COMMUNICATE WITH US

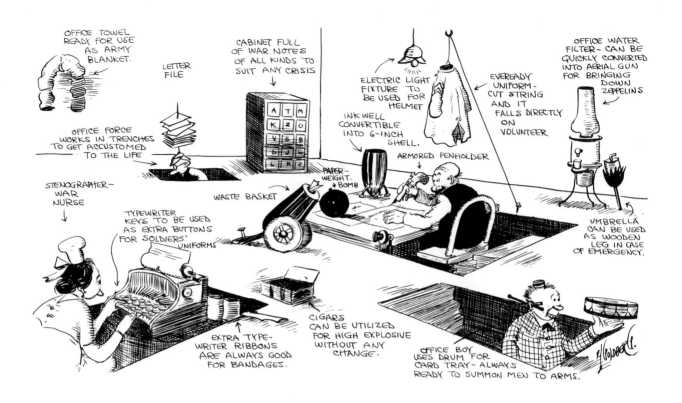

The Boob and Me

Comic art today takes in romance, adventure, philosophy, mystery, drama. It circumscribes its original purpose of burlesquing the frailties of mankind only in sufficient measure to prevent its identity as cartoon from becoming entirely lost. Of course, comics in general are still supposed to be comical; but they interpret that element of everyday life in the strictly modern manner, which is radically different from what it used to be when people would laugh hilariously at mother-in-law stories and when the slapstick was the stage comedian's one best bet.

Another thing: The principal demand of the day is for feature material which has the thread of continuity in it somewhere, whether it be through bringing in the same characters from day to day, or through the piecemeal telling of a story. By force of habit acquired in the motion-picture theaters and TV series, people have come to look for these definite personalities and for cohesiveness of action in other forms of pictorial effort which aims to amuse or entertain. The films have educated them to expect it on the comic pages of newspapers, and it doesn't make much difference whether it is there in garbled form or otherwise, so long as the reader has the pleasure of that daily meeting with an old friend, or someone quite a character.

A great many newspapers are sold largely on the quality of their comic strips. Nearly every paper of large circulation has a full page of comics, and you will notice that most of these have continuity elements. When editors try the expedient of leaving out individual comic features for several days as a means of testing their popularity, the demand of the readers most often is for the restoration of those telling stories. The comic which introduces new characters each day and does little else than illustrate a joke is the least mourned when it disappears from its accustomed position in the paper. (Naturally, there are some extraordinary exceptions to this.)

How the scope of comic art was broadened to take in emotions other than humor is exhibited by my old Sunday page *Boob McNutt.* I built up the element of romance by having Boob, a simple-looking fellow, fall in love with Pearl, a beautiful girl, who reciprocated his affection. The choice denouement, as letters from readers indicated, was to have them always on the brink of being married, with something constantly happening at the crucial moment to defer the ceremony, due to some stupid blunder by the hero. I used the device such a long time that I finally began to wonder how much further I could maintain interest without marrying Boob and Pearl. At what point would the followers of their fortunes revolt against these repeated instances of hope deferred and demand that I no longer interfere when the parson was about to tie the knot?

My readers solved this problem for me, as I had hoped they would. I began receiving all kinds of letters about the ill-fated attempts of Boob to carry Pearl off as his bride. Some of them said plainly that it was about time I developed a new story line. Others were of a pleading nature, taking the attitude that poor Boob and Pearl had been so loyal to each other that I ought to reward mutual devotion of this sort by letting them get married. Not being a hard-

hearted Simon Legree, it was O.K. with me to unite them in matrimony; but I couldn't help wondering whether the same people who were demanding this outcome would still be interested in the series with Boob and Pearl launched on a prosaic career of domesticity. "Finis" is written to most love stories when the hero and heroine join in wedlock. From my own standpoint, it was not good judgment to gratify a whim of those readers who took the trouble to write to me. There was the possibility that if everybody could be consulted the majority verdict would be the other way.

Nevertheless I took the chance, and one Sunday the followers of Boob and Pearl were given a surprise: the wedding ceremony had actually been performed. Though messages of congratulation for both them and myself poured in, including a few telegrams, I knew that only time would tell whether I was to suffer by virtue of this decision to let true love have its just reward. I rather feared that a mistake had been made and it actually surprised me to find, six months later, that the series was being received as well as it ever had.

Yet I still wondered whether this would be so if I permitted their love to run a tranquil course for good. I separated Boob from Pearl, had him living among strange people in a goofy sort of land accompanied by queer little twins, Mike and Ike. I framed an alarming circumstance that he might be forced against his will into a bigamous marriage with the fat daughter of the leading citizen. Then I received letters every week imploring me, for Pearl's sweet sake, not to let Boob commit bigamy. The world was not so permissive then of adulterated domestic bliss.

Consider what was required of the professional story-teller in earlier years. If you will look back through some of the old books you used to read in your youth, you will see that the lives of heroes and heroines moved in an even tenor and that nobody was happy if courageous Claude happened to be separated for many days

from gentle Gwendolyn. In fact, if it chanced that Claude and Gwendolyn had been lashed together in the bonds of matrimony, it was indecorous to keep them apart. Obviously, public taste has changed radically.

The *modus operandi* of an artist with a continued story on his hands may be described in a few words. His three essential characters — hero, heroine and villain — are scrambled in a series of episodes involving hairbreadth escapes, heartburnings and grotesque situations, all these adventures worked out in a serio-comic vein. For the next exploit, which goes into three or four panels if it is a daily and eight or twelve if it is a Sunday feature, he has two main points to consider — the start and the finish. The story must be taken up where it was left off in the preceding instalment and must be finished with a wallop of some kind. It makes no difference whether this climactic snapper is humorous or heartrending; the point is that it must contain some element of interest to lead the reader on.

It takes possibly four weeks or more to carry the reader through one complete episode. The nearest approach to a plot is the devising of a rough skeleton of the action of the episode and its locale. Let us say that Thornton Blake, the heavy villain, has kidnaped Ruth, Bobo's lady love. Naturally, Bobo has to rescue her in the good old heroic style, but exactly how he's going to do it, or when, is a matter to be determined by the vagaries of imagination. If enough live situations develop to prolong the agony, then it is Ruth's misfortune that she has to stay in the bad man's clutches for a fairly lengthy period; if the muse works poorly on this line, then Bobo and his sweetheart are reunited in short order. And at this point the next episode begins, to litter the path of love with more trouble. It is the irony of comic-art romance that it must travel a rocky road.

Here again is a demonstration of the public's autocratic dictation regarding what shall be accepted as a humorous situation. In bygone years frustrated love was regarded as anything but a topic capable of producing merriment. Laura Jean Libbey, Bertha M. Clay and their literary sisters used to grind out pages of manuscript on this selfsame subject, but never with the idea of making their readers laugh. The habit of the young ladies and gentlemen of that time — and the old ladies and gentlemen, too, for that matter — was to feel terribly sad about the bad breaks the heroes and heroines used to experience in their love affairs. So revered was this institution, in fact, as a tear producer that anyone attempting to burlesque it would have been guilty of a peculiarly virulent form of sacrilege. But things have changed. What used to make us cry, now makes us laugh.

But I've been wondering recently whether there isn't some kind of renaissance movement to reconstruct the comic strip into an out-and-out pathetic strip. It looks as though we were headed straight toward a recrudescence of the tear, so strong is the later-day tendency to play up the heart-throb stuff.

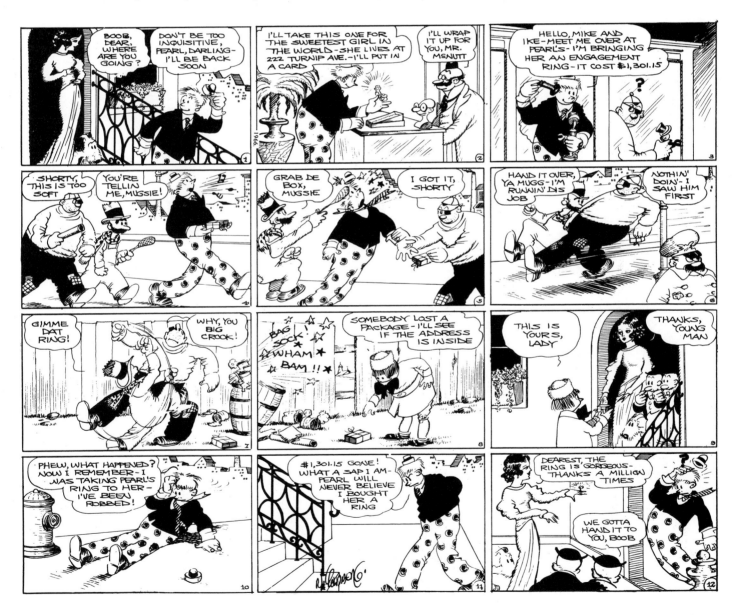

141

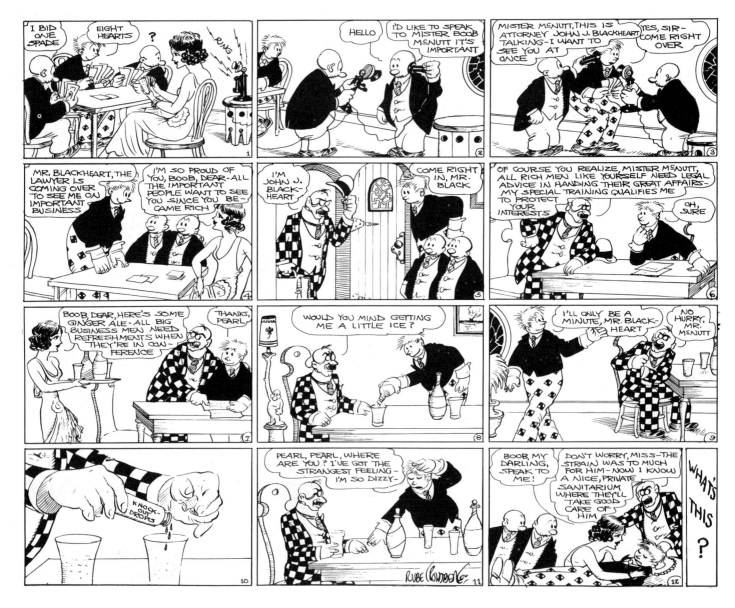

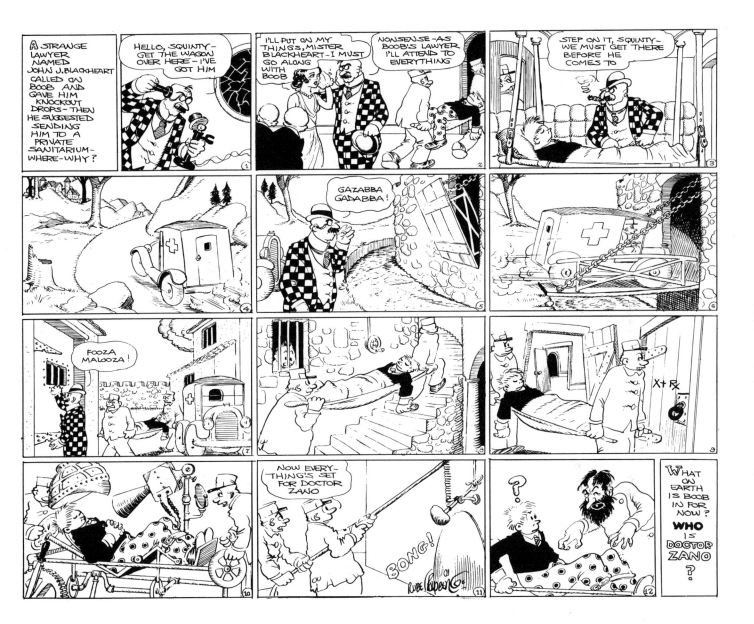

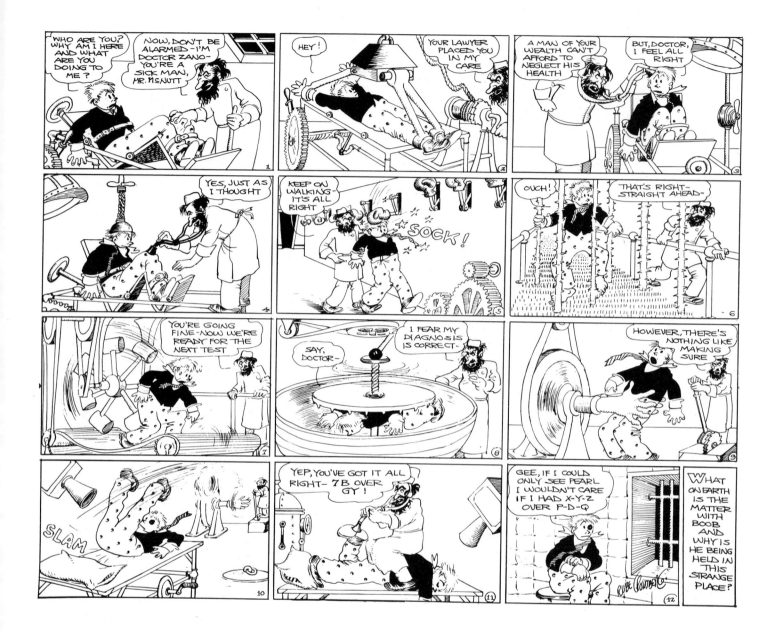

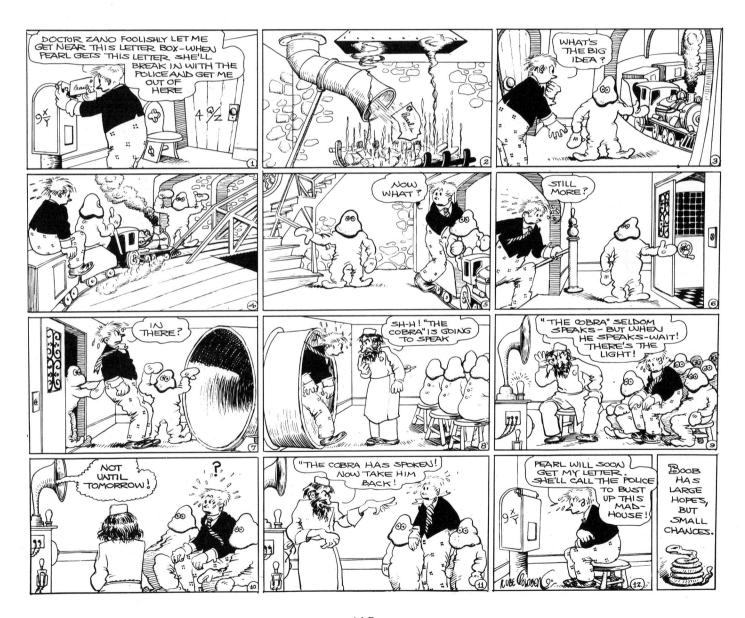

145

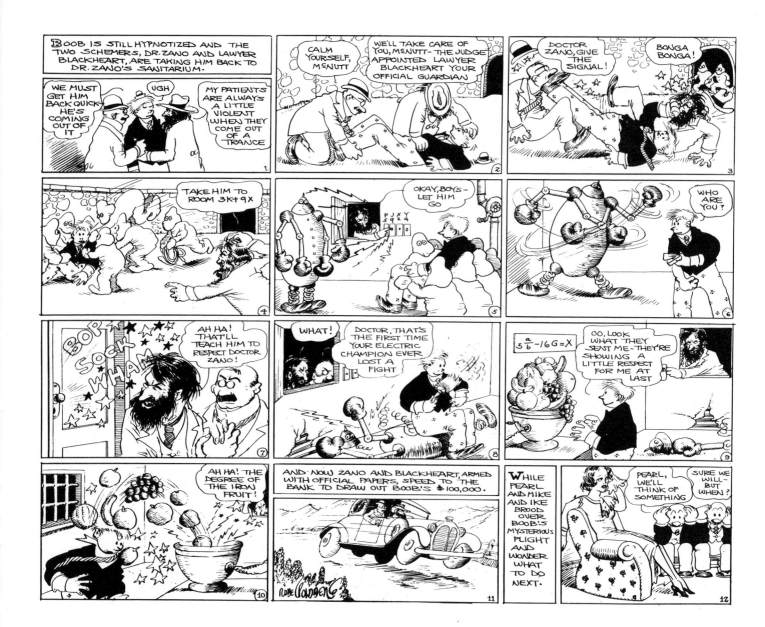

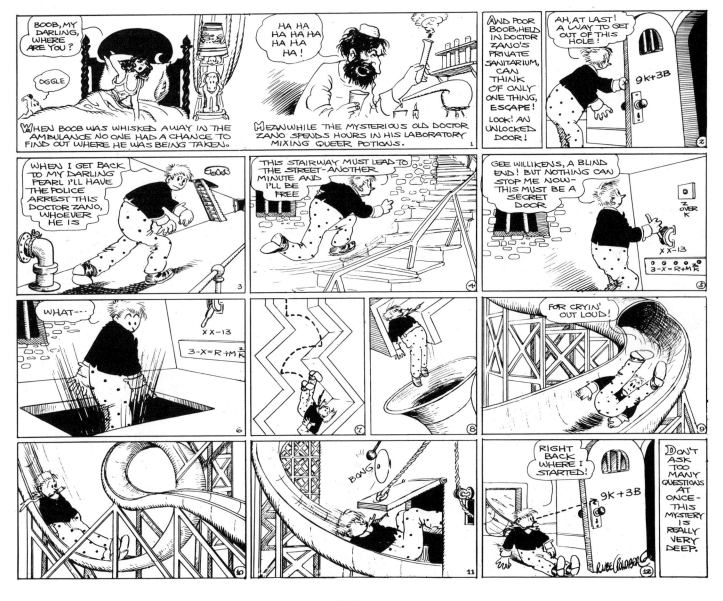

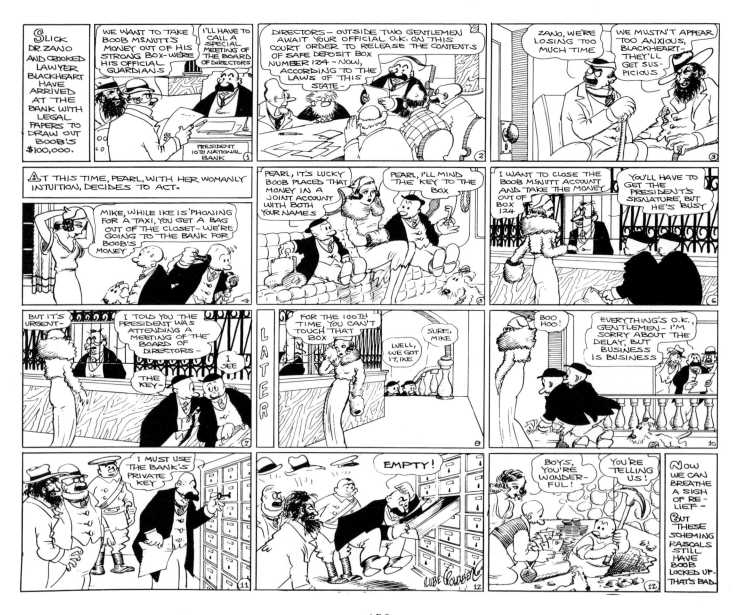

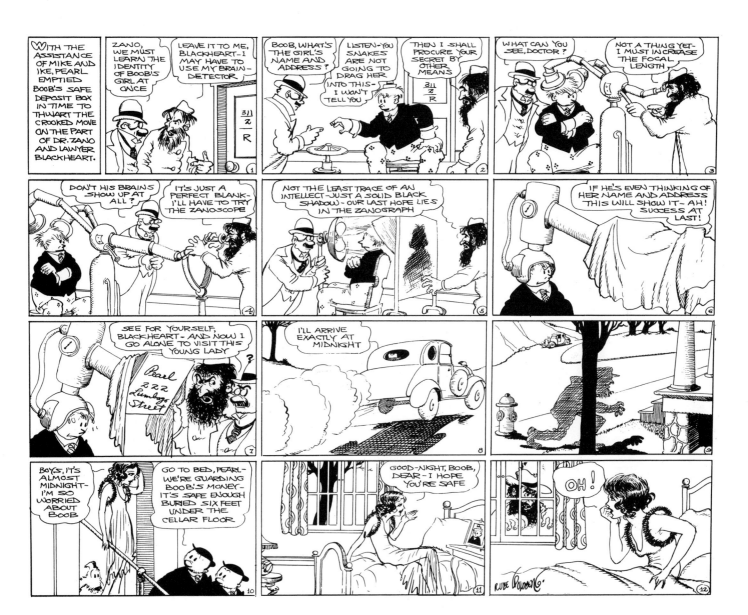

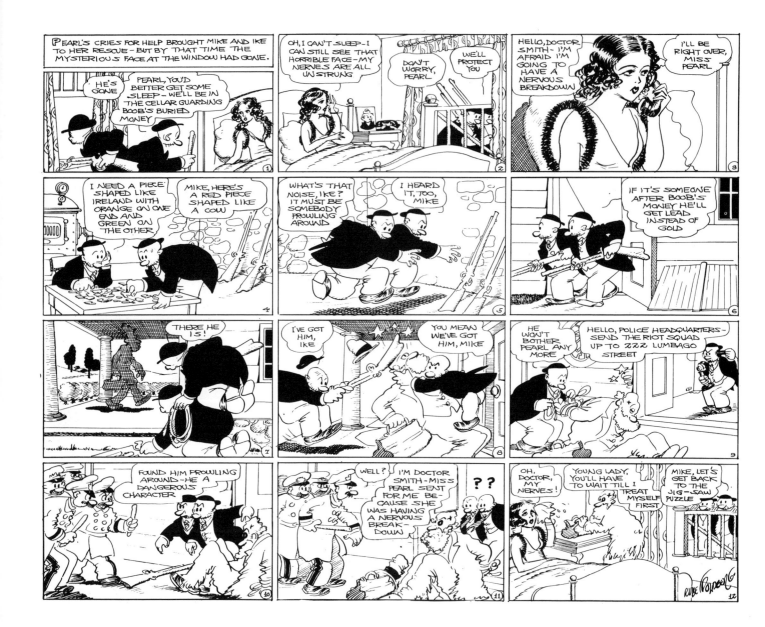

152

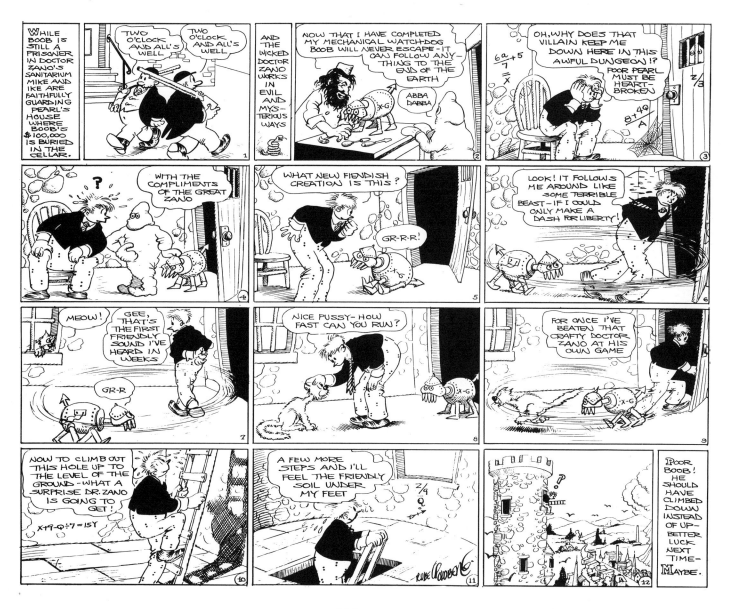

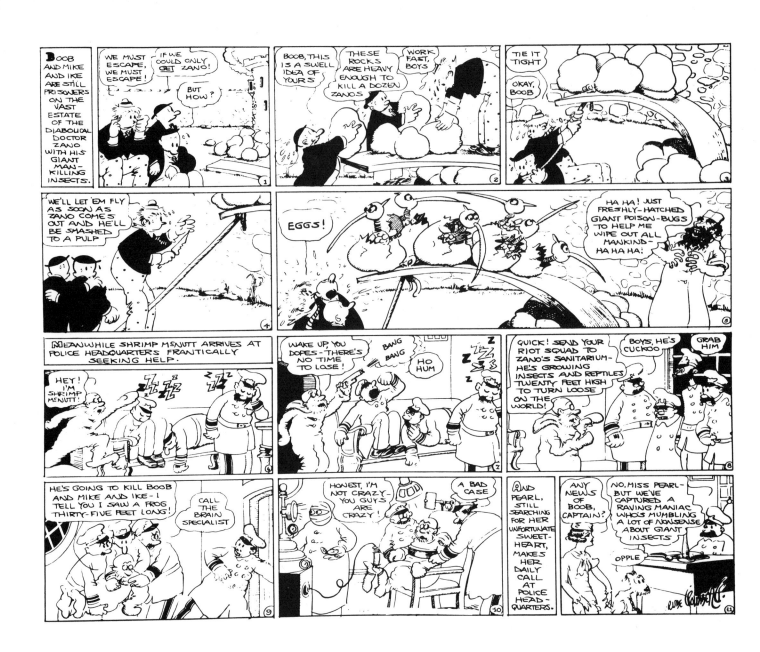

9 Mike and Ike, They Look Alike

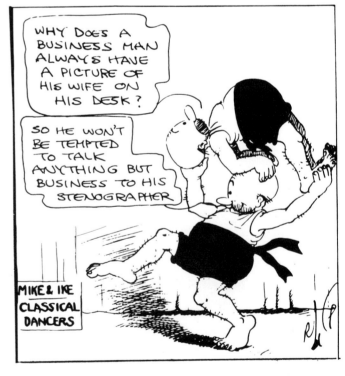

159

10

"Bill" Was No Boob

Humor is an indefinable commodity which, when you start to analyze it, may get into all sorts of paradoxical troubles. You can say it depends on timing, on mass appeal, on special ability to project the foibles of human nature or anything else you like. The test of humor is whether or not it gets a laugh, whether through the mind or through the belly. We definitely identify the result but it is hard to put your finger on the cause.

I'm not conceited when I say I've got a sense of humor; I've been living it all my life. But a sense of humor doesn't mean you're capable of being funny. I think getting a laugh is not an accidental thing. To go about it, you have to understand what's funny; to know the difference between wit and insult, between satire and sarcasm or insult.

Humor in cartoons changes with the times as in other forms of entertainment. The popular type of humor of forty or fifty years ago may seem faded and sad now even though it provoked screams of laughter at the time of its vintage. While the arrangement of pictures may continue the same, a strip, a panel or a group of loosely-connected drawings, if it lacks that 1969 flavor which is strangely present in the mind of the cartoonist, is apt to lose attention amidst the competition today.

Yet many strips are self-perpetuating. The comic strip is the only form of entertainment that is not always susceptible to the ravages of time. There usually is a capable young cartoonist waiting around to carry on, often sustaining the high quality of the original in accordance with the changing spirit of the day. This is a tribute to the fundamental vitality and general appeal of the cartoon form.

There are cartoons running in newspapers with the same characters that appeared forty or fifty years ago. *The Katzenjammer Kids, Mutt and Jeff, Bringing Up Father, Little Orphan Annie, Gasoline Alley, Snuffy Smith, Popeye* are examples. If you look up the originals of them you will find the characters somewhat different in appearance; the subject matter also. In many cases the slapstick of vaudeville has been abandoned for the milder ploy of psychology.

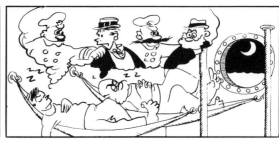

11

In Literary Moods

Hugh Fullerton, writing of me in *The Literary Digest* back in the Twenties, said, "Rube prefers writing to drawing." True. I was a happy author in the Twenties of short stories and essays for *Cosmopolitan, The American Magazine, Good Housekeeping, The Saturday Evening Post, Collier's.* One of my stories was chosen for an anthology of the best short stories of the year. Verses and song lyrics of mine were published.

In 1935, I quit cartooning for syndication rather than continue a continuity comic strip, *Lala Palooza,* I found myself hating. With relief, I devoted myself to writing, television, acting in one movie with Jack Benny, working on a playscript with my son George, until a call from *The New York Sun* took me back to the drawing board, as editorial cartoonist. I continued writing for magazines, and I published several books.

Here are some varied examples of my writing — not necessarily my best ones, because lengths had to be taken into consideration.

THEY OUGHT TO GIVE ETHER TO HUSBANDS

It was not until recently that I came to the shocking realization of the fact that women were unjustly taking all the glory for their own operations. They became suddenly renowned when they entered the hospital, and during the period of recuperation, which generally was stretched into a ripe old age, they acquired a spiritual glow that enshrined them in a niche alongside Joan of Arc, Edith Cavell and Carry Nation.

I am here to plead the case of the unsung husband who endures a sympathetic pain for every one of his wife's agonies and alone suffers the full burden of the terrific blow that comes with the doctor's final bill.

My own case is probably mild compared to those of other male martyrs of female operations. But it will serve, I hope, as a document of emancipation for obscure husband bystanders who have not received one single little flower or one soft isolated grape to console them during their period of mental travail and financial torment.

It was I who suggested that my wife see a specialist. I claim this distinction so I justly can take the credit for all the suffering which I subsequently endured. Suggesting that your wife visit a specialist means nothing more or less than a positive operation.

If a woman book-agent or a solicitor of funds for the hoarse yodlers of the Alps drifts innocently into the consulting-room of a great surgeon he will immediately order her to the hospital to be operated on for oophlitis, which does not have to mean anything at all.

An anatomical consultant need only look at a woman and she is under the ether. When my wife walked into the consulting-room of a famous diagnostician he said, without looking up from his newspaper which was open at the financial page, "Madam, you need an operation."

"But, doctor," my wife protested, "you don't even know who I am and you haven't even examined me yet."

"My good woman," he answered, as his eye rested on the latest quotation for General Motors, "you are very well dressed and that is sufficient reason why you need an operation. As far as your identity is concerned I am not the least bit interested. I only want to know who your husband is."

I call your attention to the important part I played in the transaction to counteract future evidence which seemed to point to the contrary. When she came home she told me of the interview and, with mixed emotions, both scrambled and soft-boiled, I called up the great man of medicine and gave him my bank balance.

When I reached his office the next day by appointment, I said, "Now, doctor, while I earn a nice living and am in fairly comfortable cir-

¶ "There was not a woman who called on my wife who had not had a case that was unheard-of in the annals of surgery."

170

cumstances, I am not what you would call a —"

That was as far as I got. He seized me and took my temperature, pulse and blood pressure.

"Say, doctor," I protested, "my wife is the one to be operated on, not I."

"I know it," he answered unemotionally, all the while seemingly engrossed in mental calculations. "I merely wanted to see how much of a shock you could stand."

To my great disappointment he found me to be perfectly normal and thoroughly capable of taking it on the chin. He said quickly, "Have your wife at the hospital Sunday night and I will operate Monday morning at nine-thirty."

● From *IS THERE A DOCTOR IN THE HOUSE?*, by Rube Goldberg (The John Day Company, 1929, New York).

THE GREATEST SHOW ON EARTH...
Every Four Years

Some of us who are favored by the gods become crooners. Other fortunate creatures of circumstance rise to the heights of membership in exclusive speakeasies. Still others achieve high hats and spats. But it is left for a blessed few to become part of that great national phenomenon, the Presidential convention.

Once every four years, the Republican and Democratic parties each selects something over a thousand men, instructs them to drop their saws, cleavers, pencils, trowels, boxing gloves and shovels, and hie themselves to a distant city to nominate a man to lead their party. Each of these hears the call of the crusader ringing in his bosom and feels his tremendous responsibility as he girds his hip flask to his massive loins and goes forth to fulfill his destiny of powerful righteousness.

Let us take the case of the Honorable Sumner T. Potroast, delegate at large from Pennsylfornia. A short while ago Mr. Potroast, then known only as Goofy Potroast who shellacked pretzels and turned them into umbrella handles for people who wanted something "different," noticed a crowd of queer-looking men entering his shop. He threw up his hands and told the leader to take the $4.30 that reposed in the till.

Ignoring Goofy's frightened surrender, the visitor said, "Honorable Sumner T. Potroast, I congratulate you. The people have selected you as a delegate at large to attend the national convention and name the Presidential nominee of our party. You go absolutely uninstructed, unpledged and independent. The great honor has devolved on me to hand you your credentials." Whereupon he presented the new delegate with a railroad ticket, a large black slouch hat, a badge and a cigar.

When Delegate Potroast came to, he was sitting on a train asking for another stack of chips. He listened for some comment on future procedure, hoping to be spared the humiliation of betraying his ignorance. But the coming convention was not even mentioned.

Our delegate at large entered the convention hall the following day and beheld a sight that drove the last vestige of self-assurance out of his system. The different delegations were huddled together in wooden corrals, each equipped with an elevated standard emblazoned with the name of the state represented. Hundreds of secretaries and newspapermen swarmed a main platform tearing up papers, chewing gum, and yawning. Aisles were filled with delegates picking up cigar stubs, and noises came from a series of loud-speakers on the ceiling. "That's the formal call for the convention," said a delegate at Potroast's left. Our delegate at large said he thought it was a call for help.

Then a man stood up to the microphone and talked for three hours about George Washington, Thomas Jefferson, Abraham Lincoln, the Monroe Doctrine, the Grand Canyon of the Colorado, the Constitution and the weather. Potroast at least knew that all of these were dead, except the Grand Canyon of the Colorado. But how could they be nominating the Grand Canyon for President? Nevertheless, he was anxious to cooperate for the good of the nation and told his neighbor that if that was the consensus of opinion he would cast his vote for the Grand Canyon. The neighbor informed him that the present oratorical eruption was only the temporary chairman delivering the keynote speech.

Then the temporary chairman announced that the delegates were about to elect a permanent chairman. A party may run out of ideas and slogans, but it never runs out of chairmen.

Delegate Potroast did not sleep well that night. All about him were meetings of the Committee on Resolutions, the Committee on Badges, the Committee on Handshaking, the Committee on Free Lunch, the Committee on the Mississippi, the Committee on Whiskers and the Committee on Expense Accounts. From the august deliberations that came from the committee rooms, he learned twelve new versions of the traveling-man story and sixteen new recipes for cocktails.

At the next meeting of the convention the chairman of the Committee on Resolutions read the platform, which sounded just like the keynote speech the day before. The only difference was that instead of mentioning the Grand Canyon of the Colorado, it eulogized the Rockbound Coast of Maine.

Finally came the great day of the actual nominations. Who would be the party's candidate? Did anybody know? Yes, patriot, three men knew. They were out riding in the park talking about a fishing trip after the show was over. When the speakers had fallen over from shortness of breath, the three men would tell the chauffeur to drive them back to the convention hall, and then they would pass around the word that Effingham Chowder was to be the party's choice. The three men were the big bosses — Dough, Dough and Dough.

Delegate Potroast, being uninstructed, made up his mind to listen intently to the nominating speeches. Senator Darningneedle of Virgeorgia made the first nominating speech. His voice poured from the loud-speakers like

fiery, molten lava.

"It is my great privilege to place before this convention a man, a great man, a man who is a man, a man whose home life is beautiful, a man who has devoted his whole brilliant career to public service, a man who knows no defeat, a man with the brain of a Socrates, a man with the courage of a Napoleon, a man with the soul of a Lincoln, a man who is all of a man. Fellow citizens, I now nominate a man —"

That's all Potroast heard. Pandemonium broke loose. Pandemonium is an animal that sleeps four years and breaks loose with such violence that it quickly exhausts its strength and needs four years' rest to do justice to the next Presidential convention.

Delegates jumped to their feet, grabbed the sticks containing their standards and marched up and down the aisles in hysterical joy. Potroast found himself marching and singing and shouting for everything from canned biscuits to the Panama Canal. All he knew was that somebody had nominated A MAN.

He marched around the hall for an hour and fifty minutes. One minute he found himself with the delegation from Rhohio. The next minute he was with Carolouisiana. In quick succession he trailed along with Nevadicutt, Texachusetts and Indioming. When the excitement died down, a kind fate steered him to a seat among his own delegation and he fell asleep.

Soon he was awakened by a thunderous voice popping from the loud-speakers overhead. "This is the proudest moment of my life. I appear before this convention to place in nomination a man who, as a man, is indeed a man. I wish to name a man —" The convention burst into a demonstration that made the first outbreak look like an adagio dance.

Potroast was lifted out of his seat and sucked into the maelstrom of hysteria. He marched for two hours and seven minutes and engaged in nine fights with delegates who tried to steal the banner he was carrying. It was the standard of Kansatucky, a state he had never heard of. All he knew before he lost consciousness again was that another *man* had been placed in nomination.

Delegate Potroast dozed through the dinner hour and was only aroused by the roll call of states to vote on the nominee of the convention. When the secretary called "Illirado," a delegate stood up and said, "Twenty-four votes for somebody or other." Cheering drowned out the name. When Potroast's delegation was called, the leader of the group jumped to his feet and cast the vote of the whole lot for —. Potroast tried to say a word but was socked on the head with a resolution and went to the floor.

After the nominee of the party was actually selected on the forty-sixth ballot, the delegates dashed from the auditorium to catch their trains for home. The few straggling secretaries on the platform suddenly remembered they had forgotten to nominate a Vice President. They picked up Delegate Potroast — he being the only one left — and made him the unanimous choice of the party for Vice President. The following November he was duly elected and served four years without ever finding out the name of the President with whom he shared office.

He is now back shellacking pretzels, and whenever anybody mentions a national convention he grabs a banner and marches up and down until he falls over exhausted. The curse of the delegate is on him for life.

● (From *Cosmopolitan*, July 1932, the month Franklin D. Roosevelt was nominated by Democrats to oppose incumbent President Herbert Hoover.)

FOREWARNING

We are not here concerned with the chemical mysteries of thermonuclear science with its heavy hydrogen and deuterium. Our interest lies in the visible potentialities of automation and mechanization, those fields where you can get a general idea of what is going on without being too bright.

Thousands of workers struggle each day to turn out everything from paper clips that hold together documents that nobody reads to ornamental ash trays for people who throw their ashes on white wall-to-wall carpeting. We are fascinated by the vastly complicated machines the sole purpose of which is to produce bed lamps that shed no light on the book you are reading and bone-handled carving knives that seldom make a dent in a Thanksgiving turkey.

As we move forward along the gadget-strewn path of mechanization we become more and more aware of its general theme. DO IT THE HARD WAY. The more trivial the product, the more complicated the machine.

While we follow this general theme we are not consumed with any idea of emulating some of our great industrialists who construct showy glass and steel factories in strategic spots for passing motorists to admire.

We work where the whim takes us, with no desire to impress the curious stranger. We keep our myopic eye glued to the light of integrity and pure logic. We insist, in the workings of our machines, that each operation follow the one before it in logical sequence.

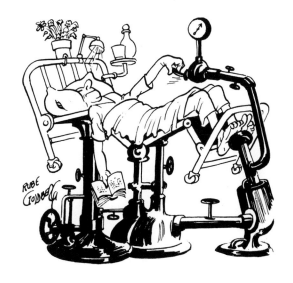

We have only one request to make of our readers. Please do not look at the final resolution until you have followed each stage in its tortuous advance toward the completion of the product.

● From *HOW TO REMOVE THE COTTON FROM A BOTTLE OF ASPIRIN And Other Problems Solved* (Doubleday, 1959).

I MADE MY BED

I was lying in the gutter outside the theater where Ed Sullivan produces his television show. I was only partly visible because it was raining pretty hard. Passers-by took no notice of me because along Broadway it is not uncommon to see people lying in the gutter with rain splashing in their faces. But I happened to emit a stomach rumble as Sullivan passed by on his way into the theater. I hadn't eaten for three days.

He looked down at me, but not in a spirit of pity or vulgar curiosity. Always on the lookout for sensational features to put on his program he thought perhaps I might be an appealing figure to excite the interest of his viewers and bring home an oft-repeated object lesson to those poor young souls who, alas, might squander their God-given endowments of talent and good fortune.

He said to me, "Young lady, you don't have to tell me. I know. You were once the toast of Broadway, an actress endowed with great beauty and a rare voice that thrilled vast audiences across the country — in theaters, night clubs, and movie houses. You had money and position, a loving husband, and birds singing on your sun porch. But like many of your foolish sisters in the profession you dissipated your blessings. You drank and took dope and went from one man to another until, until — well, until here you are lying in the gutter with rain pouring on your face and without even an umbrella to hide your shame. I want you on my program."

What he said was only partially true. I was on the stage, I did throw my life away and I broke every moral code by which decent girls are expected to live. But I was not a great beauty nor did I have a good voice. At best my voice was the sound of a rasping file on a rusty hinge. But I had a certain quality, a sensual appeal that made all my male listeners want to go to bed with me. Sure, I went to the dogs. But, boy, did I enjoy it!

I sat up with difficulty and said, "Mr. Sullivan, I can't go on your program like this. You can at least give me time to wash up first."

"I don't mean *now*," he replied in those clipped accents that remind you of the sounds that accompany the preparation of a day's supply of chopped liver in the Stage Delicatessen. "I mean for you to go on my program *after you write your book*."

I struggled to my feet, rising to a height of five feet nine in my stocking feet — I hadn't worn shoes in several months — and asked, "What book?"

"Your book, your book. I haven't time to argue now. Don't think you're any different than the rest. They all write books. Look at the money the other repentant ladies of stage and screen made out of their stories."

"Oh, those." I interrupted. "Kid stuff!"

He went on, ignoring my comment, "I'll stake you to room rent, meals, pencils, and paper. Go ahead and write. But, of course, on one condition. That you will go on my program before you accept an engagement from Steve Allen. It is a deal?"

He slipped a twenty-dollar bill into my wet hand and disappeared into the building, before I could thank him. I became dizzy with excitement. The details of my past life and all the circumstances that brought me to the plight I was in crowded into my brain. I saw my grandfather seated on his rug in the Street of the Four Caliphs in Cairo. I heard my grandmother, Bupka, wailing in her garden in Petrozavodsk after the Czar and his whole family were wiped out. There was my father, Shawn

O'Farrell, the romantic wastrel, swinging his shillelagh in Northern Ireland as though it were a magic wand summoning the banshees to play sweet music, to bring him beautiful colleens and sprinkle him with stardust laden with gold coins. All in his imagination of course when he came staggering out of McSorley's on Ninth Avenue. The drunken bum. How I loved him.

And Uncles Shamus Kaplan and Sol O'Farrell. How they lavished me with gifts at Christmastime and Yom Kippur and the Moslem Ramadan, the time of joy and fasting. And Cousin Radish Abdel Alameda, to whom I owe my education. Cousin Radish often held me on his knee in Alexandria where our summer palace overlooked the Mediterranean. I cannot attribute my rise and fall in the theatrical world to luxury or overindulgence in childhood. Nor can I attribute it to poverty. The psychiatric excuses of those others who sat in the gutter in the twilight of their careers are not for me, I am sorry to say. I was raised in both luxury and poverty. I starved, and I sated every desire.

● From *I MADE MY BED*, by Kathy O'Farrell, as told to Rube Goldberg (Doubleday, 1960) — when confessional biographies in the vein of Lillian Roth's *I'll Cry Tomorrow* were best-sellers. It was in character for Kathy to be a free versifier as well as a free lover, so —

LOVE IS LOVE

Young love is a joyous awakening
From sleep in the blanket of Time;
Where angels are singing
And clarions ringing —
A melody, pure and sublime.

The soul of the lover treads softly
O've the sumptuous carpet of dew;
There's no chili con carne
On the Lakes of Killarney,
But darling, there'll always be you.

Away with false abracadabra,
True love cannot ever deceive;
The heart may be tardy
Like Laurel and Hardy,
But still I believe, I believe!

Desire is ever a flower
With petals that welcome the day:
I'll be drinking Chianti
In gay Ypsilanti
While the birds sing their sweet roundelay.

In Rome or in staid Piccadilly
My paean of love will prevail;
I'll grow healthy and brawny
On mulligatawny
And never my passion will fail.

So my spirit will always be yearning
For thee who are deep in my heart:
May the appis in spring
Kiss the beautiful fring
And the frannam aroo never part.

● From *I MADE MY BED*, by Kathy O'Farrell, as told to Rube Goldberg (Doubleday, 1960). As indicated in other pages, these were not the first Goldbergian evocations of the Muse of Erato.

BUFFET SUPPER: Try and Get It

I was sitting in Joe's lunch wagon at about eleven o'clock at night when Mister Mooks came in. His dinner coat was mussed, and his collar was wilted.

"Hello, Mooks," I said. "What's the matter?"

He came alongside and took a seat. He said, "Whew!"

"What happened?" I asked.

"Plenty. Wanta hear it?"

"Sure. Take it easy."

"Well," he began, "I just came from a buffet supper at the Swaffers'. Before we went I told my wife I intended to get something to eat. I

said she would have to look after herself —
none of this running back and forth helping the
ladies. She said she wouldn't bother me, and she
didn't."

"Yes, yes," I put in.

"When we got there, I sneaked a look
through the dining-room door, and there seemed
to be plenty of food on the table. We stood
around for an hour or so talking nonsense about
where we were going for the summer and
whether Jean Harlow could act. There was a
fellow there who had just come back from Russia, and he told how all the people were starv-
ing over there. My feet hurt, and the woman I
was talking to couldn't hear very well.

"Time dragged along, and more people
kept coming in. I felt uneasy because the hats
and coats were piling up in the hall, and mine
were on the bottom because we came early. I
had just had my hat blocked, too. I kept waiting
for a signal to go into the dining room. After a
while I noticed the crowd beginning to surge
toward the table inside, so I knew I had missed
the signal. Unfortunately I had just told the
deaf woman that one of my boys had the German measles. She said:

"'I don't think the Germans are so mean.
You must consider their side of it.'

"I had to keep repeating it was German
measles louder and louder before I could tear
myself away. Then it was too late. The dining
room was full.

"I managed to push through and grab a
plate and knife and fork off a small serving
table on the side. All the big plates were taken,
so I got something between a butter plate and
a saucer. I stood behind some other people with
plates for some time and then discovered I was
going against the traffic and had to turn around
and go the other way. I got some olives and a
piece of celery, and there seemed to be plenty of
grape jelly, which I didn't care for anyway.

"What I really wanted was some turkey.
The breastbone was bare, but there were a few
splinters of dark meat along the side of the
platter. The two people ahead of me cleaned
these up, but I didn't feel so bad because I had
my heart set on white meat anyway. With a
little scraping I managed to get some cold beans
and spaghetti and a crust of bread that somebody had forgotten. I kept following the line
around the table without much success. I went
around three times hoping each time to spot
something new. I added a piece of lettuce and a
slice of tomato on the second round, but the
last lap only netted me an anchovy which was
left over from the hors d'oeuvres.

"Then the deaf woman came up and
grabbed the plate out of my hand saying in a
high, hollow voice: 'Oh, thanks, Mister Mooks.
It was so nice of you to get me my supper.'

"I went over and sat on a radiator, and
nobody paid any attention to me. Pretty soon
a Swedish maid came past with a tray full of
small dishes of ice cream. I reached up and
grabbed one as she went by. Unfortunately the
man who told about Russia reached up at the
same time. Our elbows collided, and the two
dishes fell on the floor. I tried to pick mine up,
but somebody stepped on my hand. I had never
been in Russia, so didn't care much about eating ice cream off the floor anyway.

"An idea struck me. Perhaps I could find
some food in the kitchen. I sneaked around
through the pantry and was lucky to find no
one in the kitchen. I opened all the little trick
doors in the refrigerator very cautiously. All I
could find was a bottle of milk of magnesia and
a wilted orchid.

"I had to go through the living room to get
out the front door. Mrs. Swaffer, the hostess,
spotted me and whispered in my ear to go into
the bedroom where a man was doing tricks for
a select group. The only trick I was interested
in was producing something to eat out of the
air. I just kept on going. I made her a present
of my hat and coat."

Mister Mooks finished his story and wiped
the perspiration from his brow. He picked up

a large menu card in a leather frame protected by a sheet of celluloid. Indicating with a sweeping motion of his hand everything on the card from top to bottom, he said to Joe, the proprietor of the lunch wagon,

"Give me that."

● From *Good Housekeeping*, September, 1935.

A drawing from *The Rube Goldberg Plan for the Post-War World,* published in 1944. I can claim proudly that my proposed solutions for everything certainly did not prolong the conflict. I designed hopefully a combination printing-press and ash-can that would have eliminated distribution of incendiary peace plans at the source.

THE CLEVER CROCODILE—

THE ACCORDION IS AN INSTRUMENT,
THAT'S VERY QUEER, NO DOUBT.
YOU PRESS THE SIDES TOGETHER
AND YOU SQUEEZE THE MUSIC OUT.
THE CROCODILE SAID, "THAT'S NOT TOO HARD
FOR ME TO PLAY BECAUSE
I CAN PUT THE THING INSIDE
MY MOUTH
AND PLAY IT WITH MY JAWS!"

DANCING ROOSTER

THE ROOSTER COULDN'T
EVEN PLAY
THE HORN OR VIOLIN,
HE COULDN'T PLAY
THE PICCOLO,
OR HARP OR MANDOLIN;
"BUT DON'T YOU WORRY, LADS,"
HE SAID,
"I'LL NOT BE LEFT ALONE."
SO HE PUT ON A PAIR OF WOODEN SHOES
AND DANCED ON THE XYLOPHONE!

THE LION IS THE KING OF BEASTS,
THE GREATEST IN THE LAND,
SO ALL AGREED THAT HE MUST LEAD
THE MEMBERS OF THE BAND.
HE HAD NO STICK TO LEAD THEM WITH,
THEY THOUGHT THAT HE WOULD FAIL,
BUT HE LAUGHED AND SAID, "IT'S ALL RIGHT, BOYS,
I'LL LEAD YOU WITH MY TAIL."

THE LION,
LEADER OF
THE BAND

THE TALL GIRAFFE
HE GAVE A LAUGH
AND SAID, "MY NECK'S
TOO LONG
TO PLAY A SINGLE
INSTRUMENT
OR JOIN THE REST
IN SONG."
BUT JUST THE SAME,
HE HELPED THEM OUT,
IN SPITE OF EVERYTHING;
A THOUSAND BIRDS
JUMPED ON HIS NECK
AND STARTED IN
TO SING.

THE
TALL
GIRAFFE

The HALF-SOLED HALFWITS

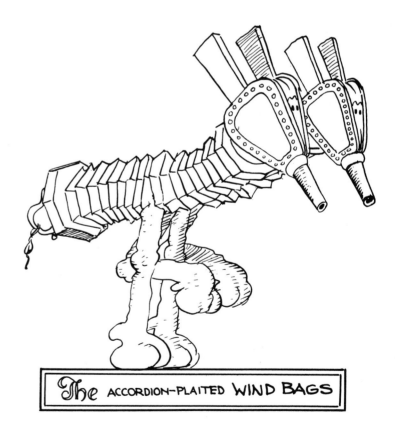

The ACCORDION-PLAITED WIND BAGS

As I mentioned in an earlier page, I wrote with Burt Grant (who did the music) a popular song, *I'm the Guy,* before Cole Porter ever thought of *I Am Loved* or Johnny Mercer *I'm an Old Cowhand.* Or, come to think of it, before Rudy Vallee wrote the words, and Leon Zimmerman the music, for *I'm Just a Vagabond Lover.*

Not content with this, I did the recitations and pictures for a *Sing-Play Color Book,* published in 1946, with music by Michael Edwards. Here (opposite page) are some of the inclusions.

This was not my first venture in zoology. As a corner "top-piece" for some of my Sunday comic pages, I originated a series of cutouts, of which you see a few at right and on two following pages.

The CHANDELIER GLOW WORMS

The HUMDRUMS

The Weeping Wuks

The PLOW-WOWS

The CLOTHESPIN-HEADED CLOP-CLOPS

The PROWLING SOOT-SOOTS

The BAG-PIPE TOOT-TOOTS

The BRUSH-FACED SKLUPS

PUT 'EM ON YOUR WALL

The LAMP-SHADE SPIDERS

180

GUT 'EM OUT!

The THIMBLE-HEADED SOCKDARNERS.

GUT 'EM OUT!

The (NORTH AMERICAN) HOOKAN-HINGES

HERE'S A COUPLE OF DOMESTIC MATES FAMILIAR TO EVERY HOUSEWIFE

THEY WERE MISSING ON NOAH'S ARK, BUT BOOB CAUGHT 'EM WHEN HE FAILED TO DUCK FAST ENOUGH

The (NORTH AMERICAN) KITCHEN VIPERS

PEACE TODAY

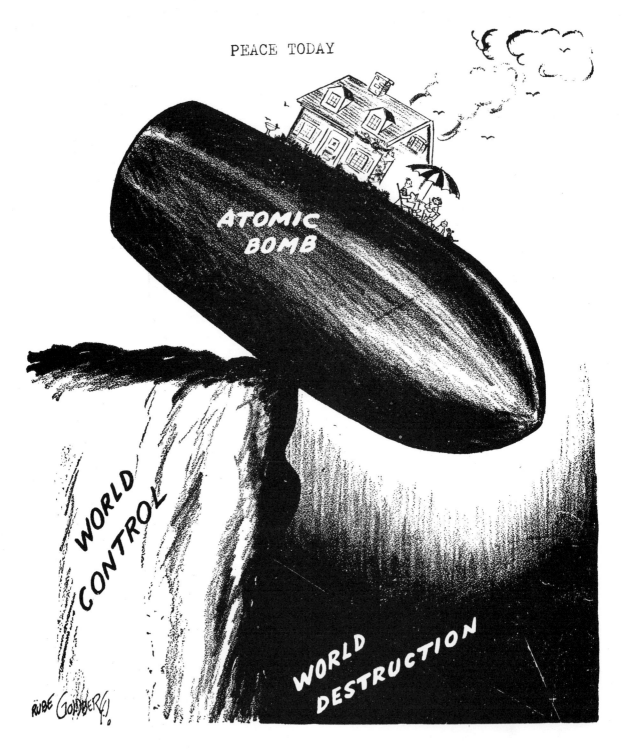

The Pulitzer Prizewinner, 1948, chosen by a national jury of newspaper editors, with the approval of trustees of Columbia University. It was in the *New York Sun* July 22, 1947.

12   On to Editorial Cartoons

Political cartoons were easier for me than the *Inventions* because they were almost pure idea, and the draftsmanship relatively simple. I could do two political cartoons a day, but an *Invention* sometimes required a week.

The political or editorial cartoon is the graphic expression of an opinion relating to current news, politics, or social injustices that may arouse public interest. It is generally printed on the editorial page of a newspaper, and sometimes amplifies the view expressed in an accompanying editorial.

Many fine illustrators have tried editorial cartooning with little success. The reason is fairly simple. The cartoon is not an illustration of a public event. Though the drawing must be executed with a certain professional artistry, the technique is merely a device to bring home a thought. The artist must direct the eye of the reader to the focal point of the idea he is trying to express. The successful cartoonist deals principally in emotions. His work cannot be pleasing to everyone. Editorial cartooning is essentially

destructive. It is an art of protest.

While Thomas Nast is generally conceded the earliest political cartoonist of influence in the United States, he had important predecessors in Benjamin Franklin, originator of the *Join or Die* rattlesnake emblem pre-Revolutionary days, William Charles, and Frank H. T. Bellew. The latter is credited with giving form in the 1850's to the popular conception of "Uncle Sam," although the term as a synonym for the Federal Government went back to the War of 1812-15 when William Charles was most active as political cartoonist.

In the latter part of the 19th century, U.S. editorial cartooning flourished in the pages of the periodicals *Puck, Life* and *Judge*. Bernhard Gillam and Joseph Keppler, two of the leading men in the field, worked on copper plates in color, and their allegorically involved cartoons were meticulously executed. Balloons (used for assumed dialogue), labels, and lettered captions were used more sparingly than they are in the 1960's. The editorial cartoons in the English magazine *Punch* preceded these by about 50 years, but they were generally incomprehensible to Americans.

Homer Davenport came out of San Francisco in the 1890's and recorded his powerful cartoons excoriating Mark Hanna and the "Monied Interests" for the Hearst papers. He gave his work a fine texture purely with pen and ink. The broad technique using heavy crayon on beaded paper, was evolved by a small group of rebels around 1912 in *The Masses,* a magazine of limited circulation strongly dedicated to political radicalism. Those men were magnificent draftsmen — Boardman Robinson, Robert Minor, Art Young, George Bellows, and William Glackens. Out of the Midwest came two men named Jay N. Darling and John T. McCutcheon, who tempered their work with humor and kindliness.

Although some papers have staff artists who sit in on editorial conferences, the practice is becoming less general due to the growth of syndication. The same cartoon can be printed around the country over a period of a week or two and still be fresh. Herbert Block ("Herblock") of *The Washington Post* and Bill Mauldin of *The St. Louis Post-Dispatch* are also represented in papers whose policy does not necessarily agree with theirs. This is a tribute to their circulation attraction.

Caricature, although a separate art in itself, is part of the equipment of the editorial cartoonist. Europeans like "Sem" (Georges Marie Goursat) and Max Beerbohm, and Americans like Alfred Frueh and Albert Hirschfeld practice the art of caricature strictly for its own sake. But the editorial cartoonist must develop skill in incorporating the exaggerated features of well-known political figures in his work. Stalin's walrus mustache, Hitler's plastered down-bang and lip smudge, Mussolini's jutting chin, Al Smith's derby and cigar, Roosevelt's eye-glasses and elongated cigarette holder were liquid gold in the cartoonist's ink bottle. When these became overexposed, along came others similarly endowed to take their place — Cas-

CIGAR AND CIGARETTE IN THE DARK—

tro's whiskers, and De Gaulle's protruding nose.

The editorial cartoon today cannot swing elections as it did in *Harper's Weekly* days of Thomas Nast after the Civil War. But it does serve as a diversion from ponderous editorials — and still has some effect in stimulating the thinking of newspaper readers.

HIS GREATEST DECORATION—

UNFORGETTABLE SOUVENIRS

AMONG THE SKYSCRAPERS

STILL HATCHING

THE GREAT UPSIDE - DOWN PHILOSOPHER -

CAREFUL, BIG CHARLIE!

VETOED!

13   My New Career In Sculpture

There was an assumption when I was eighty and had given up regular work as cartoonist that I was "retired." I hate the word. People think retirement goes along with old age. They think you just sit around counting your money or adding up your ailments or whatever; and I don't want to do that. I still have something I want to express, something to say.

I remember a conversation I had with Rupert Hughes when he was a guest on a television program of mine. Mr. Hughes was in his seventies then, with dozens of books of fiction, non-fiction, stories for children, to his credit. He was the dramatist of a number of plays, the composer of songs, the writer and director of motion pictures. I assumed that he might be slowing up. I asked what activity was now taking up his time.

He answered, "Well, I'm doing several magazine stories and working on a couple of plays and I'm doing some motion-picture script. Besides that — "

I interrupted to ask, "Rupert, do you expect to sell all of them?"

"Now, that's funny," he replied. "I really never gave that a thought."

"Then why are you doing all that work?"

"I just can't help it, I guess. I've always worked and have sold my share of stories. Besides, I get a kick out of creating something."

Here was Mr. Hughes enjoying the privilege of doing what he liked best, regardless of the fact that at his time of life he could fall back on the sedentary pursuits of old age like sitting in a rocker, or getting his hair trimmed oftener than was necessary, or waiting impatiently for dinnertime. He continued working — not from any sense of desperation, not to prove that he could compete with younger men, not because he was working against time. Mr. Hughes, I gathered, was writing for the same reason that younger men write: because he had plenty to say and liked to say it.

He continued writing when he was in his eighties. I am in my eighties. I feel that it is my privilege to speak out about that dreaded human affliction frivolously referred to as "old age."

The Commuter

I belong to a club in New York City where I seldom go because I meet there none but old men I used to know when they were all young and full of zest for their futures, men for whom those futures hadn't quite materialized and who dwell largely in the past which, through dimming eyes, has taken on an aura of glamour and excitement. They look at me and say, "You look fine," as though I had no right to look fine — as though they resented the fact that I still had most of my hair and walked with a spring in my step.

My father owned a tract of land in California in which an oil company was interested for the purposes of sinking a well. My father at the age of 93 dressed up, puffed on a clear Havana cigar, and went downtown to meet the representatives of the company. Although he was in a wheel chair he held his own with the young oil men. He was talking about the future, and nothing came of the deal because he didn't like their proposition and told them so in strong, vigorous words. His alertness amazed them. He was young with the others.

I don't believe you travel downward into the abyss of old age. I believe you travel upward until you reach a high plane where the view is clear and the whole panorama of life comes into view in the mellow light of truth and mature judgment. At 60 or 70 you don't have to exert yourself constantly to prove what a great guy you are. You have been around long enough for your friends and your enemies to know where to place you in the catalogue of human exhibits. If you have earned their respect, you are free to behave any way you like after 60 and that respect will remain. Likewise a stinker cannot suddenly sprout a pair of

wings at 60 and make anyone believe they are genuine.

After 60 you know your own capacities and limitations well enough not to expose yourself too boldly to the pitfalls of vigorous competition. You keep doing what you know you can do best, and get your satisfaction from your well-developed feeling for quality and selectivity.

You have seen fads come and go. You have seen fads suddenly return after the passing of years, bringing starry-eyed excitement to a new generation that thinks it has discovered something entirely novel and original. You have seen a whole nation act on a prediction that never came true. The years have sobered your judgment and you do not allow yourself to be swept along in the tide of mass thinking.

Your viewpoint is broad and expansive because from your position up there on the high level of 80 you are looking out on a stretch of generations, each of which is full of its own excitement. It is your special privilege to avoid a wild exhausting ride on each galloping vogue and to seek the restful shelter of the worthwhile things your experience has given you the ability to select.

I know quite a number of older men who once enjoyed success, but who have now fallen on bad times and spend most of their waking hours grumbling at the raw deal the world has given them. Age and hard luck often deal unkindly with men of mature years. But I believe that the men who got there in their younger years solely by means of superior ability will make that ability count, even become more forceful, when the years begin to overtake them in spite of a general prejudice against withering bodies and faltering wits. It must be remembered that many early successes are achieved through good fortune or special opportunity or the happy circumstances of timeliness. When these elements disappear, the fortunate creature of their machinations blames his failure on public ingratitude. He forgets that he never had very much to start with.

All you have to do is look around in the fields of art, politics, and business and you will see them crowded with people over 60 who are still forceful and active. It is their privilege to debunk the myth of old age.

Yes, illness and loneliness may come with the passing of the years. Your body starts to crack up and some of those around you pass on, leaving a void where love and mutual habit once filled your days. These are unpleasant things to think about, but they are inevitable. It takes courage to face these misfortunes. But the human soul is capable of carrying heavy burdens and can rise above them. Young people have great burdens to bear, too — the struggle to raise a family, economic problems, marital adjustments, uncertainty about their future. No people have time for self-pity.

You may not be able to keep your arteries from hardening and you may not be able to fill a gap when a loved one is taken from your side. But you can take a leaf from the book of the young squirts and liquidate self-pity by keeping busy. Raise flowers, feed pigeons, get mad at the Government, catch up on your reading, find new faces and places. Loosen your hold on the past and latch on to something connected with tomorrow.

The man of 70 or 80 can still talk young, act young, and even feel young depending entirely on what is going on in his mind, his heart, and his spirit.

What has given me a new being is sculpture.

Why did I take up sculpture? I simply got tired of the same medium for so long — fifty-nine years to be exact. I felt the urge to go back to my early love, pointing to the foibles and idiosyncrasies of people and animals around me with a satirical slant. I went to sculpture shows and become fascinated with the third dimension. I wanted to look behind the figures I created and see what was on the other side.

I bought some Plastiline (a clay with a Vaseline base that needs no coddling to keep it malleable), a modeling stand, a few tools, and went to work. I selected my subjects carefully, not in the way I had evolved the ideas for my cartoons, but with the emphasis on character, movement, and composition. Some knowledgeable people, to whom I showed my finished bronzes, recalled Daumier. I felt flattered and wondered why human comedy had not been a conscious part of sculpture since his time, a hundred and twenty-five years ago. One erudite lady called my work "literary" rather than pure form. I asked her if Michelangelo and Rodin were literary. She said, "Yes." I replied, "Well, at least, I am in good company."

Incidentally, I indicated in the beginning I was a southpaw. That is, I drew with my left hand. But I wrote with my right hand. Now I am ambidextrous in sculpture: I use both hands.

For over five years now, I have been modeling away. I have read various sculptors' analyses of their own work. Many of them exuded phrases that were ethereal and high-sounding but only vaguely understandable. They seemed to be searching for words to justify their original urge, in terms of the mind rather than the heart. They tried to explain what they did *after* they did it.

Sculpture does not need any words outside of general titles. I have no great, overpowering message to deliver. I do not want to change the world or explain its mysteries. I merely want to look at its people with you.

I sculpted the goat on a mountain peak because I liked the composition and deemed it mildly humorous. Now I hear it's a commentary on the futility of greatness and the lonesomeness of persons in high places: up there you have no place to go except down, etc., etc. I'm trying to get intentional laughs with sculpture, something I don't think is being done today. There is weird modernistic stuff, junk sculpture I think they call it — or should call it — at which people laugh. But I don't think those modern sculptors are doing this with tongue-in-cheek or from a sense of humor. They talk of "God's futility" and about "reaching for infinity."

The Climber

Waiting for a Table

Art Tour

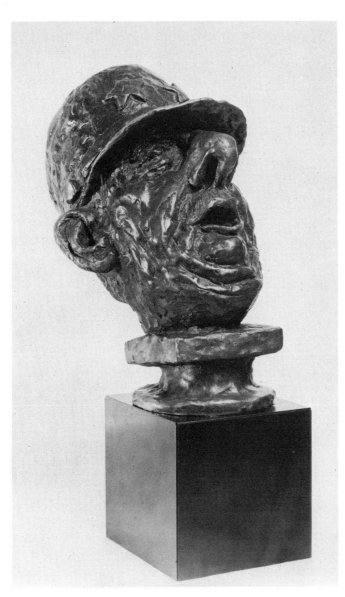

Charlie the Nose

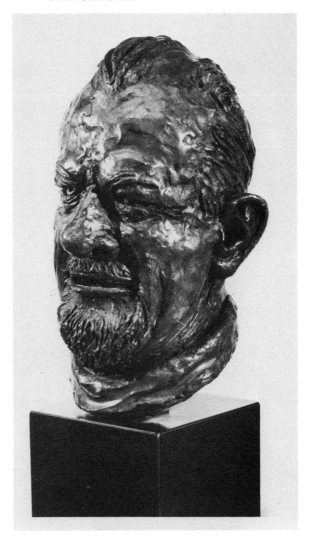

John Steinbeck

Right: The noble visage of John Steinbeck, Nobel Prizewinner in Literature. Reproduced by courtesy of Mr. Steinbeck. Above: General Charles De Gaulle of course. You may want to compare this with a De Gaulle one-dimensional caricature in page 188.

Mother and Child

Hitchhiking

196

Rube Goldberg Mouse Trap

I was persuaded to create an *Invention* as a mobile for the sculpture exhibit in 1968. It was acquired by a private collector.

A Big One

Everett McKinley Dirksen

Merry Christmas

The Rehearsal

200

Reflection

Appendix

Rise of Comic Art Up to Goldberg And Its Advancement in His Era

3000 B.C.: Egyptian cartoons circulated on limestone flakes and papyrus.

1st Century B.C.: Tabulae (tile) with satiric cartoons had popular sale in Rome. Right above: Artist depicted caricaturing a noble subject.

15th Century A.D.: Pantomimic miracle play scenes, imprinted with wooden blocks upon broad sheets and hawked at fairs, were popular picture books. *Liber chronicarium,* published at Nuremberg in 1493, depicted characters of the *Iliad* in over 1,800 blocks.

16th Century: European newcomers to America found Indians put picture stories upon wampum belts, deer skins, pottery, birch bark leaves.

17th Century: The slapstick character Punch was introduced into England from Italy, where it was of undated origin. Broadsheet representations of Punch and Judy puppet antics were sold at fairs.

Prepared by Clark Kinnaird. Portions were originally published in a pamphlet, "FiftyYears of the Comics," for the world's first traveling exhibition of comic art, 1948. A rearrangement for *The Funnies Annual No. 1* (Avon Books: New York, 1959) was reprinted without illustrations in *The Funnies: An American Idiom,* edited by Harry Manning White & Robert H. Abel (Macmillan: New York: 1963). A revision, with illustrations, was made by the author for an Italian edition of the latter (Valentino Bompiani & Co.: Milan, 1965). Further revisions and additions have been made for this book.

1754: Franklin's *Join or Die* cartoon [↓] in *Pennsylvania Gazette* did as much to effect unity of purpose in the 13 Colonies as any oratory or action before American Revolution. It became a fighting

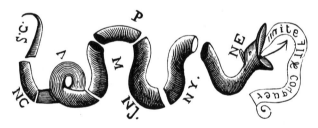

JOIN or DIE

symbol, and was emblazoned in patriot banners. Note early example of a "balloon," or sound track.

1764: Franklin, instigator of the cartoon in America, was first public man in the country to be ridiculed by its means — in attacks on his political stand in Pennsylvania provincial election.

1770: Silversmith, coppersmith, engraver Paul Revere's cartoon of "Boston Massacre" was a powerful influence in arousing American patriots to resist British government.

1779: *Paddy on Horseback,* earliest plate signed by James Gillray.

1784: Thomas Rowlandson used horizontal panel sequence, with animal characters and "balloons" to satirize Charles James Fox and Lord North ministerial coalition in England as *The Loves of the Fox and the Badger.*

1790: Francisco Goya hailed as "Hogarth of Spain."

1805: Wm. Charles, Scot caricaturist, emigrated to U.S.A. to publish cartoon plates; illustrate *American Magazine of Wit;* pen-point pusillanimity in War of 1812-15.

1809: Rowlandson created serial character in *The Tour of Dr. Syntax in Search of the Picturesque,* for *Poetical Magazine,* with verses by Wm. Combe. Publication as a book, 1812, brought demand for sequels: *Second Tour of Dr. Syntax in Search of Consolation* (1820); *Third Tour of Dr. Syntax in Search of a Wife* (1821). Meanwhile Rowlandson published *Dance of Death* (1815) and *Dance of Life* (1816), with text by Combe.

1811-16: George Cruikshank's comic genius expressed first in London magazine *The Scourge.* (He began *Sketches by Boz* with Dickens in 1836.)

1812: Enduring political phrase "Gerrymander" coined in cartoon by Elkanah Tisdale.

1813: Earliest "Brother Jonathan" cartoons engraved by Amos Doolittle. ("Brother Jonathan" was the forerunner of "Uncle Sam.")

1822: Commercial lithography established. Previously all cartoons were engraved, etched or cut on wood, copper, steel.

1823: Comic Valentines made initial appearance in U.S. — work of "Peter Quizumall, Esk."

1830: Publication of *Scraps,* David Claypoole Johnston's annual collection of comic engravings, a la Cruikshank, begun in U.S.

1831: First comic almanac in U.S. was issued at Boston by Charles Ellms

1832: Honore Daumier, leading spirit of Charles Philipon's Paris weekly *Le Caricature* [founded 1830] and daily *Le Charivari* [founded 1832], was imprisoned six months for a cartoon of King Louis-Philippe as Gargantua.

1835: Nathaniel Currier issued first of Currier & Ives lithographs, including cartoons.

1841: *Punch, or the London Charivari* was founded, an adoption of classic puppet character [↓].

1846: Comic weekly *Yankee Doodle* made its bow in New York.

"EVENTS OF THE DAY: Subscribers trying to read their papers." An Honore Daumier lithograph, exaggerating the large formats some Paris dailies adopted.

1846-47: Three novels the Swiss Rodolphe Töpffer composed as cartoon panel strips for magazine publication, were put in book as *Histoires en Estampes,* with accolade of Goethe. Töpffer introduced space travel into strips via *Le Docteur Festus,* a satire on Goethe's *Faust.*

1848: Comic weekly *John Donkey* founded in Philadelphia.

1851: *The Lantern,* humorous weekly, started at New York. Lit with cartoons by Frank Bellew, one of founders. . . . John Tenniel cartoons for *Punch* begun.

1852: Comic weekly *Yankee Notions; or, Whittlings from Jonathan's Jack-knife* first appeared.

1859: Humorous weekly *Vanity Fair* started.

1865: *Alice's Adventures in Wonderland* first published, with Tenniel's cartoons.

1870: Thos. Nast's earliest Democratic donkey cartoon appeared in *Harper's Weekly.* (However, jackass had been associated with Democrats by cartoonists since Jackson's day, originally in allusion to the Biblical Balaam's ass, 1837.)

1870: *Max und Moritz,* forerunners of *Katzenjammer Kids,* first published in U.S. in comic-book form. Rev. Charles Timothy Brooks, translator of Schiller and Goethe, rendered Wilhelm Busch's captions into English. (See 1896.)

1871: Frederick Burr Opper started as cartoonist, Madison, O., *Gazette.*

1874: Nast's first Republican elephant cartoon in *Harper's Weekly.*

1875: Livingston Hopkins, illustrator for "Josh Billings" humor, had in *New York Daily Graphic,* one of first, if not first U.S. newspaper strip with a continuing character. See [next page] *Professor Tigwissel's Burglar Alarm.* The series was given this large format.

1876: *Puck* established at St. Louis in German by Joseph Keppler. (English edition 1877.) ... Walt McDougall began cartooning, aged 16.

1880: Photoengraving introduced in U.S. by newspapers.

1881: *Judge,* comic weekly, started.

1882: Zim (Eugene Zimmerman) became *Puck* regular, aged 20. (Zim was to start pioneer correspondence school in cartooning.)

1883: *Life,* satiric weekly, founded.

1884: Vol. 1, No. 1, at London, of *Ally Sloper's Half-Holiday,* with earliest continuing comic-book

protagonist (Dickensian in character), drawn by U.S.A.-born W. G. Baxter.

1890: Alfred Harmsworth started *Comic-cuts* and *Chips* comic weeklies, in imitative *Ally Sloper* format. Latter featured tramp-errants *Weary Willie* and *Tired Tim* suggestive of Charles Chaplin character.

1891: T. A. Dorgan (TAD) joined art department, San Francisco *Bulletin,* aged 14.

Swoosh! Up comes one chicken! — A scene in an original *Max und Moritz* episode, by Busch.

1—Professor Tigwissel becoming alarmed at the frequency and audacity of burglaries, resolves to protect his own household at all hazards.

2—He lays in a stock of firearms and munitions of war.

3—He institutes a rigid system of discipline at home, and every night, before retiring, he and Mrs. Tigwissel go through the manual of arms.

4—Hearing that the Indian club is a most effective weapon in dealing with burglars, he practises upon an old suit of clothes stuffed with straw.

5—Lastly he invents a burglar-alarm bedstead (the *modus operandi* of which will be seen at a glance), and retires thereon, feeling that all is safe.

6—"Ha, an alarm! Who is it dares to invade the sanctity of the Tigwissel domicile at this dread hour?"

7—The doughty Professor arms himself with a pair of clubs, and marches forth to battle with the unseen foe, resolved to die, if need be, in defence of his life and property.

8—He meets some one in the darkness, and a terrible struggle takes place.

9—"Craven coward! How dare you assault me! I'll teach you" * * * 'Twas the silvery voice of his gentle wife, who had gone down stairs to see if the doors were all locked, and had accidentally sprung the "alarm."

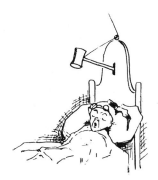

10—Professor T. reset the "machine," and is soon mellifluously breathing forth melodious snores upon the circumambient air.

11—Another alarm! "Surely that is some one burgling, burgling at my chamber door!"

12—Professor T. seizes a pair of pistols and blazes away at random.

13—His son (Tigwissel, junior, who came home late) looked in. "I thought you were up to suicide, or something of that sort," said he.

14—"I won't get up any more," said Professor Tigwissel in disgust.—"No, not if the pesky machine caves my head in."

15—A third alarm! "Oh, just hammer away, confound you! I'll not be fooled again."

16—But this time it was burglars and no mistake, and they went to work in a very professional manner indeed.

17—The next day Professor Tigwissel was somewhat out of pocket, but he considers the Tigwissel apparatus a success nevertheless, and will get it patented.

1892: Homer Davenport transferred from circus-clowning to cartooning for San Francisco *Examiner*. . . . James Swinnerton's *Little Bears* started in the *Examiner*, first continuing daily characters in a newspaper. (They became *Little Bears and Tigers* [see below] in New York *Journal* in 1896.)

1893: New York *World* published the first full-page color comic — drawn by Walt McDougall.

1894: Richard Outcault's first color comic strip *The Origin of a New Species, or the Evolution of the Crocodile Explained,* in the New York *World* [see left].

1895: *The Yellow Kid* [↓] originated in Out-

cault ¾ page, titled *The Great Dog Show in Mc-Googan Avenue.*

1896: Outcault took the *Yellow Kid* to New York *Journal; The World* had another *Yellow Kid* drawn by George Luks. The *Journal* started first complete Sunday section devoted to comics: "Eight pages of polychromatic effulgence that make the rainbow look like a lead pipe." It included *The Katzenjammer Kids,* based on Busch's *Max und Moritz* with Rudolph Dirks as first of numerous artists, and creations of Frederick Burr Opper — *Happy Hooligan, Uncle Si and Maud the Mule, Alphonse and Gaston, Mr. Dubb,* et al. (see opposite page).

1897: Opper's *Happy Hooligan* adapted into the first movie serial . . . Outcault moved to New York *Herald* to draw *Li'l Mose,* followed by *Buster Brown,* suggested by Frances Hodgson Burnett's *Little Lord Fauntleroy* (see left below).

1899: John T. McCutcheon started daily cartooning, for Chicago *Record.*

1900: *Foxy Grandpa,* by "Bunny" (Carl Schultze), began.

Eight panels of an Opper Sunday page with *Happy Hooligan, Alphonse and Gaston*. In the climax, Suzanne's father boots Happy through a window into the hands of police who are taking Alphonse and Gaston with the burglar to jail, and all four wind up in court.

1902: TAD became political cartoonist for New York *Journal*. His comic strips began 1905.

1903: Dutch artist Gustave Verbeck started *The Upside Downs*, unique reversible comic series.

1904: R. L. Goldberg's professional career began at San Francisco *Chronicle*. . . . George McManus introduced "family strips" with *The Newlyweds* Sunday page, New York *World*. . . . First daily character strip: Clare Briggs' *A. Piker Clerk* in Chicago *American*.

1905: James Swinnerton's *Little Jimmy* began, following his *Mr. Batch*.

1906: J. Stuart Blackton made *Humorous Phases of Funny Faces* animated movie series. . . . Pioneer melodramatic adventure strip, *Hairbreath Harry*, was begun by Charles Kahles.

1907: Rube Goldberg moved to New York *Evening Mail*. . . . *A. Mutt* (later *Mutt and Jeff*) started by Bud Fisher in S.F. *Chronicle*. Made into *Mutt and Jeff* in 1909. (See right.)

1909: Rube Goldberg's *Foolish Questions* published by Small, Maynard & Co., Boston. . . . Winsor McCay's animated cartoon with a continuity, *Gertie the Dinosaur*, released. (McCay was the creator of *Little Nemo in Slumberland*.) McManus' *The Newlyweds and Their Baby* (Snookums) put cartoon characters on stage (musical show).

1910: George Herriman's *Krazy Kat* evolved from his strip *The Family Upstairs* (*The Dingbats*). . . . *Desperate Desmond* made its appearance, drawn by Harry Hershfield.

1912: George McManus originated *Bringing Up Father*, with Jiggs and Maggie. . . . Rudolph Dirks moved to New York *World* to draw a second "Katzenjammer" Strip as *Hans and Fritz*. (Title changed during World War I to *The Captain and the Kids*.)

1914: King Features Syndicate established. . . . Harry Hershfield started *Abie the Agent*.

1914-18: Louis Raemakers won world renown with anti-German *Kultur* cartoons, Amsterdam *Telegraaf*.

1915: Rube Goldberg created *Boob McNutt*. . . . E. C. Segar began cartooning, Chicago *Herald*, with *Charlie Chaplin's Comic Capers*.

1916: *The Debut of Thomas Cat*, pioneer movie cartoon in color, produced by J. R. Bray.

1917: *The Gumps* created by J. M. Patterson, with Sydney Smith as first of its artists.

1919: *Barney Google* created by Billy DeBeck. . . . *Thimble Theatre* begun by E.C. Segar 10 years before emergence from it of *Popeye*. . . . Frank King's *Gasoline Alley* begun.

1921: R.L. Ripley originated *Believe It or Not*. . . . *Laugh-O-Grams*, Walt Disney's first cartoon series, made in Kansas City.

1922: Rollin Kirby first Pulitzer Prizewinning editorial cartoonist.

1923: Ernie Bushmiller's *Nancy* born as character in *Friti Ritz*, New York *Evening World*.

1924: Murat "Chic" Young produced his first strip success: *Dumb Dora*. . . . *Little Orphan Annie* started by Harold Gray, ex-"ghost" draftsman of *The Gumps*.

1926: H.T. Webster's "Casper Milquetoast," *The Timid Soul*, originated in a New York *World* Sunday page, *The Man In the Brown Derby*. . . . *Krazy Kat* and comic strips hailed by Gilbert Seldes in *Seven Lively Arts*, eight years after President Wilson read *Krazy Kat* at Cabinet meetings to relax wartime tension.

1927: Milt Gross' *Nize Baby* and *Count Screwloose* enriched popular vernacular. President Coolidge and Justice O. W. Holmes were outspoken fans of *Nize Baby* dialect characters (see top of next page).

1928: First *Mickey Mouse* sound-cartoon by Walt Disney, *Steamboat Willie*. (Two previous *Mickey* cartoons were silent.)

1929: Hal Foster put art into the first *Tarzan* strip.

1930: Disney's *Mickey Mouse* newspaper strip started. *Blondie* created by Murat "Chic" Young. (At bottom of page: the first *Blondie* strip.) . . . Harry "Abie The Agent" Hershfield starred in historic live telecast, including cartoons, from Jenkins W2XCR, Jersey City and DeForest W2XCD, Passaic, N.J. produced by Clark Kinnaird.

1931: Chester Gould started *Dick Tracy*, after penning *The Outta Luck Club* and *Penny Ante* strips. . . . First animated cartoon televised regularly: Pat Sullivan's *Felix The Cat*, via RCA field

test station, Empire State Building Tower, New York.

1932: Carl Anderson's *Henry* started in *Saturday Evening Post*. (Transferred to strip 1935.)

1934: Otto Soglow's *The Little King* transferred from *The New Yorker* magazine to Sunday newspaper comic. . . . *Mandrake the Magician* created by Lee Falk with Phil Davis. . . . *Flash Gordon* started by Alex Raymond as Sunday page. . . . Al Capp's *Li'l Abner* appeared after ghost-work on Ham Fisher's *Joe Palooka*.

1935: Rube Goldberg abandoned daily cartooning to write short stories, essays, songs, drama. . . . Fred Lasswell began long, creative association with *Barney Google* and *Snuffy Smith*. Overleaf: Barney Google with his race horse, Spark Plug. These characters uniquely inspired two popular song hits in a single year, *Barney Google* and *Come On, Spark Plug*, both by Billy Rose and Con Conrad.

1936: *The Phantom* originated by Lee Falk with Wilson McCoy. . . . Syndication of *They'll Do It Everytime*, by Jimmy Hatlo, started as replacement of the late *Tad's Indoor Sports*.

1937: Harold Foster's *Prince Valiant in the Days of King Arthur* introduced.

1938: Rube Goldberg returned to drawing board as editorial cartoonist, New York *Sun*. . . . *Superman* introduced in a comic-book.

1940: E. Simms Campbell's *Cuties* panel the first successful daily feature by a Negro artist. . . . Bill Mauldin's *Willie and Joe* cartoons originated in 45th *Division News*.

1942: *Private Breger* panels were begun by Dave Breger, originator of the term "G.I. Joe." . . .

Walt Kelly's *Pogo* created as a comic-book character. . . . First Goldberg one-man art show, New York City.

1943: Roy Crane, creator of *Wash Tubbs* and *Captain Easy,* moved into big time syndication with *Buz Sawyer.*

1945: Rube Goldberg given Sigma Delta Chi national journalistic fraternity award.

1946: Alex Raymond created his second big success, *Rip Kirby.* . . . Milton Caniff won the First Annual Award of the newly organized National Cartoonists Society, the "Reuben" sculptured by its first President. At right, the trophy and a self-caricature of the artist when he was keeping daily cartoon schedule.

1947: Milton Caniff switched from *Terry and the Pirates* into higher gear with *Steve Canyon.*

1948: Rube Goldberg Pulitzer Prizewinning editorial cartoonist.

1950: Initial appearances of Mort Walker's *Beetle Bailey,* and Charles Schulz's *Peanuts.*

1963: Tribute of National Cartoonists Society, New York, heard around world through U.S. Armed Forces Radio and Television Network.

1965: First Goldberg one-man sculpture show at Brentano's New York. (Second at Hammer Galleries, New York, 1968.) Some of his sculpture exhibited at the Montreal Hemisfair, and National Gallery of Sport, New York.

Notes:

● "Comic strips and funny papers were a natural extension of the robust humor of the 1870's and 1880's, abetted by an expanding newspaperdom, bent on circulation and experimenting with color printing." — Irving Dilliard in *Dictionary of American History,* Vol. I (Charles Scribner's Sons, New York: 1946).

● When Goldberg attended a 50th reunion of his class at the University of California, students unveiled a Goldbergian super-gadget of their own contrivance: A huge machine with flashing lights, balloons that swelled and deflated, wheels that spun, gears that meshed, pulleys that pulled, all to no purpose.

● John Hays Hammond, Jr. was an off-beat inventor and engineering practical joker. One bathroom of the guest quarters at a Hammond country-house was built as an elevator; the plumbing was rubber tubing. An unsuspecting user could be unprepared to find himself stepping from his bath into a downstairs drawing-room.

● Goldberg parodies of the Industrial Revolution have been credited with inspiring the famous Charlie Chaplin picture, *Modern Times,* and countless imitative "mobiles" and other art works.

● Peter Ustinov opined that while critics may dismiss Leonardo da Vinci's "Doodles of siege cannon and working out an extremely original solution to the traffic problem, in the end he may be remembered more for these than for that dreary Mona Lisa . . ."

● An "Automatic Hitler-kicking Machine" was included in Goldberg's first one-man exhibition, in 1942. An American, reading about Nazi brutality, got "hot under the collar." The heat set off sparks that activated a phonograph that played strip-tease music. A dancer began to strip, dropping her cloth-ing into a basket that, when weighted down, opened the door to a cage with a mouse in it. The open door could not be resisted by a cat, which, in heading toward it, unbalanced a great suspended boot so that it aimed right at Hitler's pants.

● "The great Rube Goldberg, father of Boob McNutt. He is virtually a living history of the comics from their infancy." This is quoted from George Perry & Alan Aldridge, British historians of the art. They associate its origins with Egyptian scrolls, Greek and Roman pottery, the Bayeux Tapestry — the latter they term "a remarkable narrative in comic strip form, made centuries before the *genre* had been properly invented."

● Computer machines have been found to have symptoms of nervous prostration, and to respond to rest and seclusion therapy.

● *The Evening Mail* was started in September 1867. It absorbed *The New York Evening Express* (founded 1836) in 1881. *The Mail* itself was absorbed in 1924 by *The New York Evening Telegram.*

● *The New York Morning Journal* was founded by Albert Pulitzer in 1882, a year before his brother Joseph bought *The New York World* from Jay Gould. Albert P. sold his paper in 1884 to John R. McLean, who disposed of it in 1895 to W. R. Hearst. Hearst started *The Evening Journal* in 1896. In 1902 the name of the morning edition was changed to *The New York American.* The two were merged in 1937.

● Gilbert Seldes, in a critique of Goldberg's portrayals of people, remarked: "As good is his conception of architecture and interior decoration: his endearingly ugly statues, the hideous lamps set in the middle of a balustrade, the tortured figures on which the whole edifices rest, the furniture that lacks equilibrium, are all observed phenomena, corresponding fairly to the unhappier efforts of rustic America since simple architecture and good design gave way to suburban developments and manufactured atrocities."—*The New Republic,* Vol. XVIII, No. 549.

● Pierre Couperie and Maurice C. Horn, in their annotations and commentaries for the historic 1965-66 exhibition of comic-art at the Musee Des Arts Décoratifs, Palais du Louvre, Paris, remarked that "the imaginativeness of his [Opper's] composition and caricatural style were to exercise a tremendous influence on the cartoonists of the following generation; this is particularly evident in the works of Milt Gross, Rube Goldberg, and Elzie Segar."

● By coincidence, the International Kindergarten Union in 1907 asked parents to bar comic strips from their homes.

● Rube was a big money earner in 1916, when he saw a beautiful brunette in a restaurant. He obtained her name from the manager and within a week contrived to meet the young lady. Her father headed Seeman Brothers, one of the largest wholesalers of groceries in the United States.

After Mr. Seeman found out how famous Rube was and what his income was, he was fascinated with the idea that so much money could be made simply with a drawing-table, pieces of paper, pen and ink.

● Paul V. McNutt, onetime Governor of Indiana, High Commissioner to the Philippines, Administrator of the Federal Security Agency, and Chairman of the War Manpower Commission, was quoted as saying, "Boob McNutt ruined my chances of ever being President. People just won't take a chance on a fellow named McNutt because he might turn out to be a boob."

One of Rube Goldberg's "Inventions" was turned into a surprise for him. It was entitled HOW TO GET RID OF A LONG-WINDED SPEAKER with the following explanation: "Quartet (A) sings sad song that (B) causes man to weep so profusely that his tears make plant (C) shoot up and tickle (D) bathing beauty who slides down and kicks (E) trumpeter, who waking up, gives such a blast of his horn that bystander (F) catches cold and sneezes into propeller that starts machine (G) that sweeps speaker off platform. When Mr. Goldberg was to be the recipient of an award from the Banshees Club, New York, fellow artists and a famous model acted out the "Invention" with one change. The "machine" (G) was made to lift a cover (H) and reveal the award statuette.

● In one of the short stories Rube wrote in the Thirties, *Read 'Em and Weep*, published in *Good Housekeeping*, his protagonist is an artist who concocted an out-and-out pathetic strip, *Poorhouse Peggy*. In the first installments Peggy got the measles, was run over by a truck, was bitten by a mad dog, and was beaten by a crooked lawyer named Cyrus Baxter who knew Peggy was the rightful heir to the Vanderblatt millions and wanted the fortune for himself.

The "comic" artist made a fortune for himself: "The good people of the United States took Peggy to their hearts."

● "When the 1948 election came up, Goldberg was so sure that Dewey would win that on election day he exuberantly drew two cartoons for the next day's paper. One showed a piano being hoisted out of a White House window; the other showed Uncle Sam congratulating Tom Dewey. At 3 o'clock the next morning, when it was clear that Dewey had lost, Rube was one of the most disgusted men in the world. He had no cartoon ready for this turn of events and he certainly didn't feel up to drawing one congratulating Truman. Instead he had three words set in tiny type in the ocean of white space usually filled by his cartoon. They said: 'Rube Goldberg regrets.' This was one of the best laughs in the post-election crow-eating which most commentators, columnists and pollsters had to do. President Truman sent for the original and had it hung in his White House ante-room.

"Not long afterward Goldberg, along with other members of the National Cartoonists Society, visited the White House. President Truman singled Rube out, saying, 'Everybody knows Rube Goldberg's stuff.' Rube glowed." — Harry Henderson in *Pageant*, Jan. 1951.

Books by Rube Goldberg

Foolish Questions. Boston: Small, Maynard & Co. 1909. Reprint of panels from the New York *Evening Mail*. Inscribed "to my friend Franklin P. Adams, who made this book possible."

Chasing the Blues. New York: Doubleday, Page & Co., 1912. A collection of cartoons and Goldberg "verses" from the *Evening Mail*.

Seeing History at Close Range: The Experiences of an American Cartoonist While Marooned in France During the Outbreak of the Present European War. New York: Morris Margulies. 1914.

Is There a Doctor in the House? New York: John Day Co. 1929. (Three editions.) "A brace of scientific studies by this noted Specialist, to wit: They Ought to Give Ether to Husbands and What You Need is Exercise." "Respectfully Dedicated to the Doctor Who Blighted My Wife."

The Rube Goldberg Plan for the Post-War World. New York: Franklin Watts, Inc. 1944. Dedicated "To All Other Planners for the Post-war World."

Music in the Zoo: Pictures and Recitations by Rube Goldberg; music by Michael Edwards. New York: Mills Music Co. 1946.

Rube Goldberg's Guide to Europe, by Rube Goldberg and Sam Boal. New York: The Vanguard Press. 1954. "To Irma and Francesca and all the other wives who never get a chance to have a book dedicated to them."

How to Remove the Cotton from a Bottle of Aspirin and Other Problems Solved. Garden City, N.Y.: Doubleday & Co. 1959.

I Made My Bed, by Kathy O'Farrell as told to Rube Goldberg: The Superconfessions of a Superlatively Naughty Girl. Garden City, N.Y.: Doubleday & Co. 1960.

Soup to Nuts. (A movie.)

Play: *Day of Rest* (with George W. George).

Sculpture Exhibitions: Rube Goldberg's Human Comedy, at Brentano's, New York; and Hammer Galleries, New York.

Goldberg cartoon series:

Lunatics I Have Met
Foolish Questions No—.
I'm the Guy
No Matter How Thin You Slice It, It's Still Boloney.
The Inventions of Professor Lucifer Gorgonzola Butts
Phoney Films
I Never Thought of That
The Weekly Meeting of the Tuesday Women's Club
I'm Cured
Slackers
Joe, Sweep Out Padded Cell No.—.
Boob McNutt
Mike and Ike, They Look Alike
Brad and Dad
They All Look Good When They're Far Away
They All Come Back for More
Is There a Doctor in the House?
What You Gonna Do With It?
This All Comes Under the Head of Pleasure
If Plays Were Only True to Life
People Who Put You to Sleep
Blame It On Wilbur
Little Butch
Sideshow
Life's Little Jokes
The Candy Kid
Steve Himself
Benny Sent Me
Bill
Lala Palooza
Telephonies
Animated Cartoons (1916)
The Drawing Game (Tv: 1948)
Pepsi & Pete (for Pepsi Cola)